Heart First

Book #2

Heart First

A ReAwakening

Michelle Miller

Prologue

When I left Costa Rica, I hadn't realized that psychedelics would no longer be an active part of my life, at least not like they once were. It was as if those experiences, especially my NDE (near death experience) when I almost drown while swimming on magic mushrooms, needed to simmer and to assimilate. *If* I was processing the information I was presented with on my psychedelic journeys, it was something that was running in the background of my everyday life that I was completely unaware of. I became entranced by the speed of life, tic-tocking like a pendulum at an ever-increasing pace. The pressure of my *(our)* business and endless to-do lists had me hypnotized and focused solely on physical reality. Every once in a while, I would break free and become conscious. It was as if I would come up for air, I'd look around and wonder where the magic had gone and why it was no longer available to me. Then, life would call. I'd take another deep inhaling breath, and while holding it in, I would immerse myself once again.

Contents

Chapter 1

Act Like You Know

I had shoved off from Costa Rica and landed in Quito, Ecuador on a one-way ticket for the first time ever, alone with no guidebook and no idea where I was going. My heart was wide open to infinite possibilities, just as it had been on so many adventures in my past. Although now as a massage therapist, I had a career I could take with me anywhere and I hoped to extend my travels by working or volunteering somewhere long term.

Four months prior, I had left my home base on Kodiak Island, Alaska with the intention of traveling or *living* abroad indefinitely. I packed up the rustic oceanfront cabin I rented for years and put most of my belongings into a storage unit. I also sold my car and gave up my massage office where I had run a successful business. Even though Alaska was a special place, I was ready to experience more of the world, for as long as possible, and thought that maybe in the process, I would find somewhere to put my roots down.

I had landed a job in Puerto Viejo, Costa Rica, and I really loved it there, but my vision was fluid, and my ninety-day tourist visa was about to expire. My ideal scenario included staying and working somewhere for a few months until I felt it was time to move on or another opportunity presented itself. I thought that maybe I could circumnavigate the entire continent of South America this way, and from there, who knows where. Europe? Asia? India, perhaps.

As I exited the Quito airport, I wanted to look as if I belonged there. This was partly out of fear of not wanting people to realize I didn't have any idea where I was going, and partly because I had a raging case of tourist denial. I did not want to look like an outsider *or* be treated like one. No. The purpose of this trip was not to stay in party hostels and meet fellow travelers. That hadn't even occurred to me. I wanted to live like a local, to meet Ecuadorians, and to experience their culture. I wanted people to think I *was* Ecuadorian, or in the very least, that I lived here, that I belonged here, and that I knew what I was doing.

It was 2003, so there were no smartphones at this time, though I could have gone to an Internet Cafe while I was still in Costa Rica and researched places to stay prior to my arrival here, but I did not. Throwing myself into the unknown and seeing what presented itself had been a key element to my adventures ever since I had declared myself a student of The Universe nearly ten years ago when I dropped out of college after only one semester. In the past, I had traveled within the U.S. and Latin America, sometimes with no money what-so-ever. So, this time around, with a few thousand dollars in savings, a career I could take with me, and an emergency credit card, it felt like all the security I needed.

In an effort to avoid the multitude of airport taxi drivers harassing every potential customer, I inhaled a huge dose of confidence and crossed the busy street in front of the airport to wait for the public bus. Even though I'm a Caucasian woman, my dark hair, almond shaped eyes, and olive skin *do* help me pass for Latina. However, in contrast to the well-dressed Ecuadorians living out their daily routines standing around the bus stop, my large backpack, colorful hippie attire, and clunky Birkenstocks screamed *turista,* which I was completely oblivious to in that moment. I had paid for private Spanish lessons in Costa Rica, so by this time I was present-tense-limited-fluent in Spanish, if there is such a thing. It was enough to understand people's concerns for my safety as they began to gather all around me. "*Para donde vas?*" "Where are you going," they asked as a group.

"To the center," was my reply as it seemed like the most logical destination. I figured there must be a big church and plaza in this capital city center with lots of reasonable hotels. I expanded, "I'm going to a hotel in the city center."

"What hotel?"

"*Hotel Central,*" I lied, determined to maintain the appearance of knowing where I was going and thinking surely there was a centrally located hotel with some such name.

Various people shook their heads and wagged their fingers pointing me back towards the airport telling me to take a taxi. "*Peligroso* (dangerous)," they said.

"Hmmmm," I squinted as the wind was taken out of my pseudo-Ecuadorian sails.

I slowly turned around and begrudgingly headed back across the street working on my new storyline for a future taxi driver. Now, I included a protective layer to my story and some reassuring landmarks. I was going to meet my (fictitious) boyfriend at Hotel Central, right near the main church and plaza. My previous travels had taught me that this scenario existed in all major Latin American towns; a plaza, near the main church, where there had to be a hotel. But as my driver approached what I assumed was the downtown area, he repeatedly questioned me about the exact name of the hotel. *"Geezo* buddy," I thought. "What's it to you? What are you, a taxi driver or something? If you don't know where Central Hotel is, then shame on you. You should know where every centrally located hotel is!"

As we circled a large church and plaza for a second time (my landmarks that I also didn't know the name of), his increasing frustration was apparent as he seemed to become more aware that I was unsure of where I was going. In order to get out of the taxi, I finally had to concede that maybe I had misunderstood my boyfriend. As I paid this man and began to prepare to step out onto the street, what I had perceived as his frustration suddenly changed to real concern. He warned me that this was a dangerous area and that I shouldn't walk alone there at night. I reassured him that the hotel had to be near here, as said boyfriend's directions were, "near the central church." I thanked this skeptical man telling him I would check with my boyfriend now as I slammed the door shut making a note-to-self: taxi man that I had lied to in order to ensure my safety was actually highly concerned for my safety and wanted to help me. I found my way to a very basic cheap hotel where I stayed for three nights while I acclimated to Quito's altitude of 10,000 feet above sea level. Once I got my bearings, I bought a small cheap guidebook in this seedy section of the city.

Although this area of the capital city was rough around the edges with the streets littered with garbage and emanating a septic-type smell, it didn't seem that dangerous during the day. The people I passed on the street were friendly, always returning my greetings or answering my questions, but even still, I did follow the taxi driver's instructions. I ate dinner at simple restaurants just a few doors down from the hotel *early* and was sure to be back in my room just after dark.

Now that I was actually here and moving about in the third world, I began to realize just how cushioned and tailored for tourists Costa Rica had been. There had been maps, street signs, buses, shuttles, English spoken, guides, activities, expats, tours, etcetera to help me on my way. The fact that Costa Rica is considered a developing nation was becoming more apparent, and the extreme poverty I was seeing in Quito made the larger middle class in Costa Rica obvious. In fact, my time spent there was now feeling like Disneyland when compared to this bustling and dirty city with a population of 1.5 million people, which in the area I was in, provided no tourist information what-so-ever. Not that I minded. This was exactly the type of authentic experience I was seeking.

As I walked down the street, I was taking in how people were dressed, especially the small children with their brown skin and rosy cheeks who were bundled in flannel shirts and tiny jeans. They walked alongside their mothers, holding their hands as they slowly navigated the litter on the sidewalks and the gaping sewer holes that had broken or missing grates. I loved looking at the small newspaper stands that sold a variety of winter beanies and scarves for this cooler climate along with mints, gum, and snacks. I ducked inside a few small convenience stores to see what was available. I was fascinated by what people ate, what they used to wash their dishes and clothes, and the different names used for fruits and vegetables since Spanish varies from country to country. I loved observing how people interacted with one another; their customs and mannerisms, the different tones, and the expressions used. Just being in the mix of all of this felt like I was in an altered state or a living meditation. There was nowhere I had to be. I could just be present, observing my surroundings and engaging in each interaction I was presented with. I was open to any and all opportunities, feeling into what my next destination would be.

I sat on the hotel's dirty burgundy and gold tasseled couch in what was considered the lounge area, but it actually felt more like a Latin grandmother's living room. I paged through my tiny guidebook wondering what my next move would be as fellow guests opened and mixed individual packets of instant coffee (which was surprisingly the norm in this coffee producing country) with the hot water that was provided. They greeted everyone, which I saw was customary when they entered a room. Prior to leaving Alaska, a friend had recommended a village in Ecuador that she thought I would like. I remembered her saying it was the textile capital of the country, but I had forgotten the name. As everyone gravitated to the large wooden table where a fruit bowl with apples and bananas sat alongside the dry cookies that were available twenty-four hours a day, I listened to their conversation, mostly understanding that they were there for either work or local tourism. I began to engage from the sidelines. "*Sientate*," they told me, motioning for me to join them at the table. Soon, I was asking if they had seen more of the country and if they had any travel recommendations for me. They were all staying in Quito but said Otavalo seemed to be the place everyone went. "*Para el mercado* (for the market)," they added. "*Mucho turismo*."

This was the second time someone had recommended Otavalo, and now with the mention of the market, I figured this was probably the place my Alaskan friend had told me about. All signs were pointing to Otavalo.

The following morning, I boarded the bus, excited to leave the city and to see what was awaiting me on this next stage of my journey. I looked out the window at my new surroundings mesmerized as we passed the actual line of the equator and headed northeast out of Quito through what looked to me like the high desert at the base of the Andean Mountains. The vegetation became more and more sparse, giving way to open plains, farmland, and grazing animals.

At one point, the police stopped the bus, boarded, and asked to see everyone's documentation. When I asked my neighboring passengers what was happening, they whispered, "*Control, Colombia*" and "*Narcos*" making me realize for the first time just how close I was to the border of Colombia and how real the cocaine trade actually was. "Hmmmmm, would that be my next destination," I wondered.

If I was going to circumnavigate South America, Colombia could be a quick and easy start! I thought about my strait-laced parents, especially my mother who had a tendency to over-worry, and I knew that they would focus on the negative press Colombia had received in the past for kidnappings, the cartel, and the cocaine trade. They would absolutely shit themselves if I went to Colombia on my own.

Otavalo was very tourist friendly, and I was finally able to find a vegetarian meal that consisted of more than white rice, beans and a slice of tomato, which I *did* appreciate. I found a cheap room not far from Poncho Plaza which I later discovered is considered the largest market in all of South America. For me, this was one of the advantages of not over researching and over planning and the luxury of being on an open-ended adventure. As I saw it, having little to no expectations allowed me to remain wide open to receive magic such as this world-renowned colorful labyrinth which came into my life as a complete surprise. Traveling this way, I found myself in a perpetual state of awe and gratitude for the unforeseen gifts that were presented to me.

As I began to bounce from stall to colorful stall I hummed the Grateful Dead lyrics, "Some folks trust to reason, others trust to might, I don't trust to nothin', but I know it comes out right."[1] I smiled at, greeted, and chatted with the vendors, feeling naturally high as I touched their beautiful alpaca wool sweaters, scarves, wall hangings, bags, jewelry… it was endless! As an artist myself, I admired all the colors and complexity of their handiwork. I noticed that nearly all of the vendors were dressed in their traditional Kichwa clothing. The men were small but strong in stature, and could be seen hunched over, hauling huge bundles of textiles on their backs. They wore blue or gray ponchos, white calf-length pants, rope sandals, dark felt hats, and a

---

[1] Grateful Dead, "Playing in the Band," Track #4 on Skull & Roses Live Album, Warner Bros., 1971, Vinyl

long braid down the middle of their backs. The women wore intricately embroidered white blouses along with woven black skirts, and shawls. I marveled at how much they seemed to have preserved their culture as they spoke their indigenous Kichwa language to one another.

Eventually, I began to expand my exploration by venturing into neighborhoods following various cobblestone and dirt roads. I absorbed the view of the unanticipated Imbabura Volcano and the click clacking of simple looms as people weaved in their homes with their doors open to the breeze of the fresh mountain air and the happenings of their neighbors. Most of their homes were modest, made of painted mud with terracotta roof tiles and decorated with colorful flowers. Many had dirt floors, and both men and women sat on low stools inside working on their looms.

These traditional looking people blew my mind when I began to notice them loading their huge bundles into brand-new four-wheel drive pickup trucks. They had to use the oh-shit handle to hoist their small bodies into the driver's seats of these oversized vehicles. Then, slamming the door, they sped off creating a cloud of dust which shattered any preconceived notions I had of *all* of these indigenous people living meek or poverty-stricken lives. Clearly not everyone had flashy cars here. But when I began to notice multiple "Export" and DHL shipping signs in the shop windows, I realized how industrious they actually were, doing business all over the world. A light went on for me! My friend Debra, whom I had worked for in Alaska, had told me to let her know if I saw anything of interest for her import store on my travels, saying that she would possibly have me do some shopping for her store or come down to join me. I loved the rainbow colors of *all* the textiles, and some of the sweaters were only $6 or $8. They were perfect for Kodiak. In fact, I had seen these same sweaters being sold in the artistic town of Homer, Alaska for $30 or $40, and some of the more expensive ones were priced at $70 or $80! It looked as if the Kichwa people were set up to ship to anywhere in the world, so it seemed like the perfect place to tell Debra about. The next time I hit an Internet Cafe, I wrote to her with details about the market, the products, and the prices and decided I should wait for her reply before I moved on. I also wrote to a cute blonde California surfer dude I had met in Puerto Viejo, Costa Rica to see if he could get worked into my travel plans again at some point in the future.

Just when I felt like I had seen most of the town of Otavalo, I crossed paths with an incredible looking long haired Mexican *young* man. He was selling stones and his jewelry, just as I had done in the not-so-distant past. We made a great connection and talked for a long time. He eventually invited me to go to the sacred grounds at the Peguche Waterfall with him the following day. I was twenty-six years old but having dated and lived with a plethora of partners that had no future potential, I had told myself that I was now looking to meet someone who was more financially stable than a street vendor living out of a tent. But as I looked at this young man with his gorgeously classic Native American features, all the little voice in my head was saying was, *why not.* He had jet black long straight hair, a perfect face with beautiful high cheekbones, light brown skin, and a thick three stranded bone choker around his neck. He was gentle, there was definitely some mutual attraction, and this was a good opportunity for me to practice my Spanish, or so I told myself. Fully aware that I was now about to embark upon a fling without any future sustenance, I agreed. Then, we never really separated to meet up the next day. He stayed with me at my hotel, which didn't disappoint, and the following day, we stopped by his tent (which was at a hostel) for him to gather and leave some of his belongings on our way to the waterfall. Just like the market the ceremonial grounds, hiking trails along the creek, and the actual waterfall itself were a complete and welcomed surprise.

When we arrived, Santiago (or Santi) pointed out the large sundial on the ceremonial grounds where the annual Inti Raymi festival was held on summer solstice. In his broken English, and using my basic Spanish, I understood that he had recently observed a smaller celebration for the spring equinox. As we walked past families at the picnic tables and started up the trail towards the waterfall, I took in the smell of the forest and the tall eucalyptus trees as well as Santi's teachings. He was explaining the importance of the water and how the purification baths are a part of the sun worship and ritual of Inti Raymi. When we arrived at the waterfall it was beautiful but crowded. We made our way up a little higher than the crowd, taking in its power, mist, and the incredible sound from its fifty-foot drop.

We continued on away from the entrance hiking for some time until the trail opened to a valley with the river at its center. We stopped to smoke some of Santi's seedy weed, which intensified the natural beauty and magic that I sensed all around us. Santi told me how special this area is, pointing out the irrigation systems running below the stone paths that were built in pre-Columbian times. He told me about the community of people that still reside in this part of the protected forest who manage the park and the tourism in this area. He explained that they are modest people who we would probably see bathing or washing their clothes in the river. He advised me not to gawk or take photos, but to respect their privacy. As we walked in silence, I felt as if I was on psychedelics. I realized that this was the first time I had ever walked in the forest of South America, and I began to feel so much gratitude for my guide and such a special introduction to this part of the world. I became acutely aware of my every step and of each person we passed on the trail. I could feel the energy of the trees and hear the sound of the river. There were couples and families sitting, lying, or playing in the grassy field. Some of them were sprawled out on blankets waiting for their clothes to dry on the riverside rocks. We passed a few elders walking on the trail in their traditional clothing with rope sandals on their weathered feet and their long braids swaying as they used a walking stick to help navigate what I imagined was their main means of transportation. At some point, I thought we would probably turn around and head back the way we came, but Santi knew the way to another village and how to catch the bus back towards Otavalo.

I stayed that night in Santi's tent, but the following morning, knowing this would be (and should be) short-lived, I opted for some alone time again. I told him I wanted to regroup at my hotel and then get myself to an Internet Cafe to check if I'd be doing some shopping for Debra before I traveled again. To my surprise, she had said she was coming to Ecuador to meet me. She had already purchased her airline ticket. She would arrive in Quito on

Good Friday, which was about three weeks away. A rough plan began to form as I typed my response to her stating I would get to Quito before she departed Alaska to book a room and let her know where to meet in the city.

Prior to having my massage business, I had worked with Debra in her cute import/bookstore which was full of Alaskan artwork, clothing, jewelry, rocks, crystals and findings from around the world. She was eighteen years older than me, so we considered one another sister-mother-daughter-friends. I was super excited to see her, to shop together for her store, and the fact that she had included a couple extra days for travel time after.

Since I would be returning to Otavalo in three weeks' time, I was ready to move on and see more of Ecuador. My next and last day in Otavalo, I went to see Santi and told him my planless plan to leave for I-don't-know-where. He suggested we leave together the following day and that I come with him to Baños, a small tourist town centered around the hot springs and the Tungurahue Volcano. I happily agreed to him being my temporary hot new travel partner on this course that was unfolding for me.

It was a full day's travel from Otavalo back to Quito and then on to Baños together. Once we arrived, Santi introduced me to a lovely German woman named Alma who was working to build a nearby orphanage. I expressed my interest in possibly volunteering within her project, but she reassured me she was still in the preliminary stages which was currently more focused on meetings and funding. Even so, seeing so much poverty in Ecuador was beginning to make me doubtful that I could find work here as a massage therapist, so volunteering somewhere in exchange for room and board seemed like it may be a lot more plausible. This was my first and *only* potential volunteer opportunity I had stumbled upon thus far, so I filed it away towards the top of my brainscape knowing I could absolutely imagine myself working with orphaned children. This was exactly the type of meaningful, *rewarding* project I was looking to be a part of.

Alma and Santi were losing me in their Spanish conversation as they excitedly caught up with one another. It seemed as if he may have a place to stay with her at her house, and I didn't want to impose. So I thanked them both, telling them I was going to explore Baños some more and look for a hotel. Alma was gracious and apologetic. She told me I was welcome any time and suggested I come back later, or possibly for lunch the following day. I thanked her and Santi, truly feeling grateful to them both. And like that, I said goodbye and was happy to be on my own once again.

Chapter 2

Tigrita

Though I did have lunch with Santi and Alma the next day, I now felt committed to spending more time on my own, soaking up the energy of the hot springs, and the picturesque town of Baños. I enjoyed the large community style pool of the hot springs that sat perched on the steep hillside, alternating between floating on my back and taking in the views of the town below or the stunning waterfall above. The town itself was full of small souvenir shops, Internet cafes, tour offices, hostels, and hotels. I began to pop inside tour offices and then onto the Internet in an effort to organize the one thing I knew I did want to see; the pink river dolphins and the blue and yellow macaws. I signed on to the cheapest jungle tour I could find on the Napo River, which is a tributary to the Amazon River. The most affordable way to get there was an eight-hour bus ride that actually took eleven hours. The majority of the trip was driven on a dirt road to the town of Coca (yes, Coca), which is also the name of the plant cocaine is derived from.

There was a noticeable difference on this bus ride without my male travel companion. I was now subject to multiple men on the bus attempting to strike up conversations with me. They usually started with, "Are you traveling alone?" and then moved to, "Are you married?" and finally, "Do you have any children?" By the end of the bus ride, I was beginning to fabricate a new story for myself. "Yes, I am married, and have six (later twelve) children, but my husband understands that I love to travel." Their inquisitive faces would change from shock, to disbelief, and then laughter, realizing I was messing with them. I was thankful when the driver put the movie Anaconda on which was very fitting considering our final destination. I could then practice looking extremely engrossed in something other than the male attention I was receiving.

I stayed one night in the hotel that the tour company suggested. In the morning, I met my other group members who were three young Ukrainians; two men and a woman. All three were well dressed; the men in polo shirts and khakis, the woman in a nice red and white dress with matching white shoes and purse. The two guys were doctors, a fact they shared with me prior to even their names, and the woman was introduced as "Antin's wife." As we all shook hands, I asked and pronounced their names slowly, hoping to remember them, but as Viveca reluctantly offered up her hand, she looked away while rolling her eyes. I empathized with her having been introduced as "Antin's wife" as if she had no personality of her own, but I wasn't into her perceived attitude. Symon, the unmarried doctor, broke the tension by shaking my hand and introducing himself. "We all call her Vivi," he said smiling, seemingly the friendliest of the three.

We chatted about their arrival via airplane versus my long day on the bus, and Antin was quick to point out that I was, "*Only* staying three nights in the jungle," whereas they were staying five. The hotel concierge told us that our guide would be late and instructed us to reorganize our luggage and get any last-minute supplies or breakfast while we waited. We all stored our unnecessary luggage at the hotel, and I waited while they discussed their next move. Vivi complained that it looked like you, "Can't even get a decent cup of coffee in Coca." Antin suggested they try, and I opted to hit the streets. I invited Symon to join me thinking he might want an Antin-and-Vivi-free opportunity. "Where to?" he asked as we left the hotel, turning onto the sidewalk.

"I dunno, we could get a smoothie from a fruit cart if you're hungry," I suggested, telling him I got one the night before. A little skeptical, he finally agreed to *todo* (everything) while we stood on the curb in front of the expectant, smiling smoothie maker. *Todo* meant yes to the fruit, yes to the protein powder, yes to the honey, the bee pollen, and to the mini Cornish eggs. Everything was looking good as the fruit cart owner gleefully added all his ingredients, until the eggs went in; shells, bits of nest, poop, feathers and all. We both exchanged a shocked, wide-eyed look as the vendor continued to smile reassuringly. "*Prueba lo* (try it)," he said to Symon grinning from ear to ear as he handed him his drink.

Symon reluctantly took a sip from the straw, and then reassured the man that it was very good, offering me some. "No thank you," I responded, adding in English, "I'm vegan, I don't eat bird poop." Symon paid this nice man and as we walked away, we both began to laugh uncontrollably. When we were finally able to catch our breath, he accused me of completely misleading him. I defended myself saying I had no idea that bird poop was included in *todo* because I hadn't ordered mine with eggs. He actually took a few more sips before throwing it away unfinished, and we made our way back to our point of departure.

We all loaded up in a 4x4 truck with our guide Manuel and leaving the hustle and bustle of this large river port town, we headed towards a simple dock and a motorized dugout canoe. We spent over an hour in the wide Napo River and then turned and headed upstream in a smaller branch of the river and into dense jungle. It was slow going as the small motor fought the current to get us to the lodge. We were barely making any headway as I took in the thick canopy of trees, vines, and the sounds of the birds and insects.

Once we arrived, Manuel showed us to our extremely basic rooms which were made with rustic wooden planks elevated over the mangroves. Then we were led to the outhouses, which I hadn't even thought to look into when I booked the tour. Vivi's outward objection confirmed that they hadn't noticed the bathroom description or lack thereof either, but I remained silent, just taking everything in. There was no water the first night. No water for us (nor the cook) to wash our hands or to clean the piles of dirty vegetables that lay in crates atop the open-air kitchen's wooden floor. Our guide made up for these inconveniences with his sense of humor. After dinner he told us that malaria was extremely prevalent here and as a precautionary measure, we should share a bottle of *medicina* or medicine together. He explained that because malaria affects your liver as does alcohol, tequila is the best natural preventative to counter malaria. He didn't have a bottle of tequila, but instead Cristal, the Ecuadorian alcohol made from sugar cane that he was going to share with us. I thoroughly enjoyed Manuel's good spirit and the ability to practice my Spanish with him, but the Ukrainians were not amused. The doctors began to object to his science, pointing out that normally people who get malaria have to limit their drinking or it may cause a relapse, "if not properly treated." Manuel just laughed, shaking his head no and reassuring us that this was, "*La mejor medicina* (the best medicine)."

He poured a tall shot in the only shot glass he had for us all to share and offered it up to me first saying, "*Verdad Tigrita*?" This translates as isn't that right Little Tiger, which apparently was now my new nickname. Enchanted by his positivity and my endearing new name, I chugged the medicine and passed the glass back to him asking, "Why am I Tigrita?" As he handed the next shot to Symon, he turned to look me in the eyes saying, "Because you are traveling all alone as a woman, Tigrita. That is very brave. Like a tiger." I smiled, glowing in his acknowledgment. Vivi countered this with a long, annoyed sigh and pushed on the picnic table to rise up from the wooden bench as she announced she was going to bed. "But you haven't had your medicina yet," Manuel said unphased, holding out the next shot to Antin. One look at Vivi told us all that Antin had better join her, and he excused himself politely saying, "Maybe tomorrow," wishing everyone a goodnight. Symon and Manuel continued to drink, and I listened as Symon picked Manuel's brain about anacondas, the mosquito population, and tomorrow's order of events. When I walked off to bed, I had the classic Wizard of Oz song in my head, "Lions and tigers and bears, oh my."[2] This was partly an outward expression of how pleased I was to now be a tiger but was also due to my excitement for the possible wildlife we could see the next day.

That night I began to feel like I was getting a cold. Through the sparse planks I could hear my single Ukrainian friend sniffling and sneezing in the next room. Before long, I was in the bathroom with diarrhea (presumably from the lack of water and the dirty vegetables), hardly sleeping between trips to the toilet and blowing my nose. In the morning, my spirits were still high, even though I had incredibly low energy as I hiked with my cheap poncho on in a steady rainfall. I took in the vegetation of the tall trees and the jungle vines as Manuel taught us about the many uses of the plants all around us -- dyes, food, medicine, and even communication. He explained how the giant Ceiba grandmother tree is now comically called the telephone tree, demonstrating how their elders used to use large sticks to beat on their huge elephant like buttress roots to communicate with the neighboring tribes or other hunters. I was fascinated by all of this, but if Vivi and the doctors were too, it didn't show. They kept asking Manuel what their chances of seeing animals were in the rain. It was a bit disappointing I admitted to myself, but I wondered why they were so bummed when they had four more days left. Surely they would see *some* wildlife during that time. *It's day one, for God's sake!* Their negativity encouraged me to keep my mood elevated, but now I felt feverish, had a sore throat, and was super tired. As we stood under the grandmother tree in the rain, it became increasingly more challenging to not focus on my health, the weather, and the swarm of mosquitos all around us. In fact, now I

[2] Vidor, King, et al. The Wizard of Oz. Metro-Goldwyn-Mayer (MGM), 1939.

was sure my symptoms were actually malaria. Towards the end of the hike, I walked with Manuel, confiding in him that I thought I had malaria. He burst out laughing and reassured me, "You cannot have malaria Tigrita! There is a two-week incubation period." Even though I felt silly, I still knew I had something. When we got back to camp, I forfeited lunch and laid down trying to regain some energy for our afternoon river adventure.

I now had a full-blown cold, but it was raining less as we went purana fishing and we *did* see the pink river dolphins surfacing their beautiful pink-gray heads to spout water right by the boat! The following day, when we saw the blue and gold macaws fly overhead as we paddled upriver, I looked to the sky thinking both of these sightings were *my* good omens. It was as if I was being rewarded for trying my best to keep up my morale and seeing these colorful birds squawking in pairs overhead brought me back to a sense of gratitude for this amazing planet and the energy I always felt I received while I was in nature. In contrast, my tour-mates were now grumbling about only having seen one small anaconda (the main thing on their bucket list) as well as the lack of amenities back at the lodge. Clearly, they were out of their comfort zone, but I had a hard time empathizing with them because for me comfort was an illusion, or in the very least, precarious and subject to change. Historically, I had purposely put myself in challenging situations because I knew this was where growth happened, where memories were made, and lessons were learned. When I felt challenged, it was a call to rise above, to find a new perspective, create change, and make the best of it.

These three whining and complaining served as reconfirming evidence that just because you had money or so-called success, it did not mean you were necessarily happy. I didn't see three professional people struggling in uncomfortable circumstances. I saw spoiled *rich* people who couldn't appreciate the beautiful nature we were in or simply accept what is. In my mind, they were suffering because they were too dependent on exterior factors to bring them joy or comfort instead of generating happiness from within. This was exactly why I refused to buy into the American dream and why I had left the U.S. indefinitely. Because not only did I know "Money can't buy me love" or comfort, I also knew it was buying a whole of other things back at home such as war, inequality, and morality for huge industries such as oil, agriculture, and big pharma.[3] So instead of fighting a system I didn't agree with and against values that I saw as misaligned, I preferred to remove myself from it altogether. I no longer wanted to be an accomplice by paying into something I didn't believe in. I wanted to get off of the machine, escape the ordinary, and find my own way to live an extraordinary life. For me, this was being a "Soul Rebel," and I took Bob Marley's lyrics if you're "not living good, travel wide" to heart.[4] So here I was, attempting to travel wide, and not only did I prefer planning less, I also preferred to live with less. That was one of the main reasons I enjoyed traveling in Latin America. The people here seemed to be much wealthier in the happiness department even though they had fewer material possessions. Still, seeing as I was going to be leaving the jungle the following day, I

[3]Lyrics from Beatles song, "Can't Buy Me Love," track #7 *A Hard Day's Night*, Parlophone (UK) & Capitol (US), 1964, vinyl

[4] Bob Marley & The Wailers, "Soul Rebel," track #1 on *Soul Rebel*, 1970, Trojan, vinyl

had to admit I *was* happy with my current exterior factors. I could tell that Vivi now envied me for what was previously viewed as "*only* a three-night stay."

I braved the long bus ride again, meeting more curious male acquaintances as I alternated between telling the truth and new fictitious versions of my marital status. It made me sad to think that I probably shouldn't outwardly express all the high happy energy I was feeling. One of the main reasons I was here was to have intercultural exchanges with people, but undoubtedly my openness (smiling at and greeting everyone) was bringing about too much unwanted male attention. I looked to the local women on the bus for social direction and they all seemed stoic, bored, and even annoyed by the bus ride unless they encountered someone they knew. This was not who I was. It made me angry that I needed to dim my light so that my friendly curiosity would not be misinterpreted as flirting. This was essentially the same roadblock that my NDE (near death experience) in Costa Rica, as well as the use of psychedelics, had presented. It was knowing and feeling excitement because there was more to reality than meets the eye, that we are all connected to source, and that all things are possible. But it was difficult to know what to do with this information. I wanted to "express myself," and quite literally like N.W.A.'s remix it was, "crazy to see people be what society wants them to be."[5] I wanted to sing about free will and unconditional love from the mountaintops but was constantly confronted with the fact that sadly, speaking your truth and exuberating pure joy for life wasn't socially acceptable behavior. And in this environment, it was clearly bringing about the

[5] N.W.A. "Express Yourself," track #8 on *Straight Outta Compton*, Ruthless Priority, 1988, vinyl, CD, cassette

wrong assumptions. For safety's sake, I felt I had to suppress (at least some of) the expansive love light of the universe that I felt was coming through me. Instead of smiling and greeting everyone with enthusiasm, I alternated between having my head in my book and looking out of the window concealing my passion for life. I told myself this would be my own spiritual/social psychology experiment of sorts. I was putting "As Within, So Without," to the test, seeing if this inner shift could affect my outer journey.[6]

[6] Teaching from the ancient Hermetic text *The Emerald Tablet* thought to be authored by Hermes Trismegistus

Chapter 3

WhoKnowsWhere, Ecuador

The large Guayaquil bound bus was beginning to descend towards sea level, making hairpin turns on the fast-moving highway switchbacks. The lush green hillside and the steep drop took turns alternating which side of the bus they were on, all while oncoming traffic whizzed by. We were passing and being passed on sketchy sections of the road, which made me question if this bus wasn't going to be the vehicle transporting us to an *actual* death experience. Having seen the mountains and the jungle, I was now headed towards somewhere not-yet-decided on the coast. As I traveled, I continued making a conscious effort to contain my excitement, though now with this more life-threatening bus ride, my attention had moved from observing social behavior to other esoteric lines of questioning. Someone once told me that they thought fatal plane or bus crashes were the result of collective karma. I wasn't exactly sure what that meant, but this seemed like the perfect context in which to ponder this theory. I asked myself why out of all the people in the world, these particular souls had come together to travel today, trusting this particular bus driver to hurl us forward into our seemingly individual realities. I pictured how small the bus actually was in the grand scheme of things, imagining it as a tiny dot moving on our huge green blue sphere of a planet that is spinning in outer space. I wondered if collective karma meant we had all been in past lives together and had made some horrible collective decision in the past. Did it mean that on some level the majority or all of us have decided we are okay with dying today? *Why didn't I know more about karma?* This was precisely the type of spiritual thinking that in the past, if I wasn't careful, could become overwhelming. I imagined this was why so many people distracted themselves with media, materialism, or other people's stories; as an effort to avoid experiencing a complete existential crisis. I decided it was best for me, and for the group, to not focus on us collectively deciding to die together. Once we were down the mountain and I was no longer at risk of becoming carsick, I put my head back in my book.

Not too long after, I felt a gentle tap on my shoulder. I turned around to see a teenage girl in a school uniform sitting in the row behind me. She asked me where I was going, in English. As I peered between the crack in the green pleather seats, I opted for the truth this time. I told her that I didn't know. "To Guayaquil, and then to the beach, somewhere." She told me I was welcome to stay with her at her dad's house in Guayaquil. We continued to chit-chat through the seats. She told me she was fourteen and studying English, would love an opportunity to practice her pronunciation, and that I could stay the weekend with her and her family. She rattled on and on until the woman sitting next to her eventually stood up and motioned for me to take her seat so that the girl, whose name I discovered was Mary, and I could carry on our conversation side by side. She rattled off the names of a number of beaches which I took mental note of, and by the time we arrived, I knew all about her father, stepmother, and half-brothers. She had convinced me to catch another bus with her to their *Guayaquileño* neighborhood.

As we made our way out of the city towards suburbia the simple cinderblock homes that were built right alongside of one another and whose windows and doors were covered with wrought iron bars, slowly began to have more space in the yards. After walking a few blocks from where the bus had dropped us off, we arrived at Mary's two-story track home in a modest middle-class neighborhood. Just as she had promised, her family completely welcomed me. I loved seeing how they lived. The house was decorated with as much gaudy lace as seemingly possible (on the tables, bar countertop, and over plain colored curtains) along with an unreasonable amount of family photos on the walls. Mary finished introducing me to her family and then showed me to her teenage room which was cluttered with posters of animals and boys, photos of her and her friends, clothes, a cute heart shaped jewelry box, and remnants of childhood toys. It was much like any young American girl's room. As she began to ask me questions and share more with me about her fourteen-year-old life, her age and immaturity became apparent. But it occurred to me that by curbing my enthusiasm on the bus, I *had* attracted a more meaningful and benign intercultural exchange, one that unknowingly was precisely what I had hoped to receive.

The first night I was there we all walked to a local street fair together that was just blocks away from their house. It was like a neighborhood block party but with rides, games, and food. Her brothers rode the mini worm roller coaster and paid 25¢ to race battery operated toy cars (the kind every American child has) in the street. I marveled at their excitement of jumping on a regular trampoline and we finished the evening eating cotton candy, talking, and laughing with one another. The second night (after a bit of Mary probing her parents which I sensed had to do with the cost), we all piled into a taxi together, her father directing the driver to Malecón.

Once we began to walk along the wide Guayas River on a beautiful red and yellow brick boardwalk, her father became more animated explaining that Malecón is one of the largest urban renewal projects in all of South America. He pointed out all the playgrounds, monuments, statues and gardens that the project had included and marveled at the fact that many other people and families were out enjoying the boardwalk. He explained how dangerous and dilapidated this had all been just a few years ago. It was as if he still couldn't believe it as he shook his head and said, "You could not have walked here without being jumped, robbed or worse."

Later, we made our way through crowds of local and foreign tourists, up the iconic brightly painted stairs of the Cerro Santa Ana hillside. There were colorful homes, little shops, cafes, and restaurants on either side of the steep cement stairway. Once at the top, we took in the amazing view of the riverside city from the church perched up above. I offered to treat everyone to an ice cream on our way back down, which they refused, paying for mine instead. As the two boys bounced down the stairs ahead of us, I imagined them as the active expression of the joy we were all feeling. Seeing this made me think that maybe I didn't have to outwardly express *all* of my enthusiasm for life. As a deep sense of gratitude came over me for this family and experience, I thought that maybe allowing myself to inwardly bask in this glowing feeling could be enough.

I would have loved to have seen the Galapagos Islands while in Ecuador, but I knew this was out of my budget. Instead, I continued my journey to the coast following Mary and her family's recommendation to what I'm assuming was Montañita Beach, but honestly, I'm not sure where I actually was. There was only one or two hostels there at that time, a handful of hotels, a few local bars and restaurants, and one window store on the beach. The kind of place where people rode horses down the beach for transportation. I found a cheap private room with a shared bathroom in one of the only hostels just a block off the beach, and my first night there I shared a communal dinner that the owner of the hostel had cooked for a group of her guests. I didn't get a good vibe from this woman, and at first, I gently refused her dinner offer of a reasonably priced shrimp plate, telling her I was a vegetarian. Through a strange looking forced smile, she said she could accommodate me and that there was, "nowhere else to eat in the village." But once I agreed, she served me up a saucy dish of shrimp curry anyway. That night, I became violently ill, out of both ends, all night long. There was a really sweet South American artisan hippie traveler that I had been chatting with earlier that day and at dinner who heard me, and during one of my trips from the bathroom back to my room, he handed me a bottle of water and some soda crackers.

"No one else got sick," the snarky Caucasian owner remarked when I officially emerged from my room some thirty hours later, telling her I thought it was the shrimp. I thought it could have been the shrimp, the vegetables, or the water they were cooked in that I was not used to. The fact that this woman had used high pressure sales to get me to eat her food and then had been so unaccommodating with my diet, made me wonder if something about me getting sick wasn't intentional on her part. I was still sick days later when I met a young indigenous guy (only nineteen years old) Armando on the beach. He told me about his grandparents who lived in the mountains who cultivated and used lots of medicinal plants and suggested we go there to their *finca* (farm) together. He was also an artisan, sweet, and persistent, so when I felt well enough to travel, it seemed like this was to be my next destination.

We boarded a bus together, but this time there is no way for me to know where I actually was. We were in the highlands, in the central southern area of the country. If I had to make an educated guess, I'd say it was somewhere in the south of the Azuay Providence, because the names Nabón, Pucará, and Girón all look vaguely familiar. It was a very rural area of Ecuador and took a good part of the day, probably about four buses, plus walking up a dirt road to get there.

Armando's grandparents welcomed us with open arms, but they did not live on a farm by anyone's standards. They were simple people, traditionally dressed, her in a cream-colored peasant skirt, he in capri length pants, both with little sweaters, felt hats, and braids down their backs. They lived on a small lot with surrounding neighbors that had a one room dwelling with a dirt floor where they slept. Grandma and Grandpa were so happy to see Armando with a girl, a "*gringa*" no less, that they set to work on killing one of their best roosters for dinner. I explained that wasn't necessary since I was a vegetarian and had a bad stomach. Armando kindly reminded them that we had come for natural remedies for my stomach. All of this went by the wayside in the midst of their rooster chasing excitement. Once caught, Grandma slit his throat and squatted down at the spigot (which was their only source of water) to set to work preparing water for rice and defeathering what would be dinner. I also saw her squat to pee in the yard, so I assumed there was no bathroom for my still churning stomach which was now somewhat under control with the help of Imodium. These people were so poor I think they only had one bowl, so I was served first. They sat and watched in anticipation wanting to see my reaction to eating their best chicken. Feeling horrible, I explained I was vegetarian, I didn't eat chicken, and I shouldn't try it with my *estomago malo* (bad stomach). Armando, now angry, began yelling at his grandmother telling her we had come for natural medicine for my stomach. Throwing his hands in the air, he demanded that she make me some tea. Both physically and emotionally exhausted, I ate as much white rice as I could before I passed the bowl along to Armando to share the untouched chicken.

Grandma and Grandpa had one bed made of bamboo sticks with straw for a mattress. They prepared their bed for Armando and I, laying the only blanket they owned atop the straw to provide extra cushioning for us. They spread hay on the dirt floor in the furthest corner for themselves and slept there on top of plastic woven sacks. As I lay there, in this extremely uncomfortable situation, all I could do was plan my departure for the following morning as I reminded myself that I had no idea where I actually was. As I tried to replay the bus rides in my head backwards,

Armando's arm found its way across my body. I promptly removed it, turning my back to him, my side pressing into the hard bamboo frame. I was being bitten by mites. This was the cycle that repeated itself all night long. Planning escape, arm, removal, hard bamboo, mites, mites, mites. Though I didn't think I was in any real danger, I couldn't believe he thought I might have sex with him while his grandparents were lying on the floor beside us. "*Alto*" (stop), I told him loudly at one point, hoping I *did* wake up his grandparents. I pictured the red octagon of a stop sign that I would see from the bus when I left the first thing in the morning.

As soon as we were up and moving, I told Armando he needed to help me leave. He agreed to this, walking me back up through the village and then down a steep dirt road in the forest that we had not walked up before. As we traversed together, me walking with my backpack and smelly black Birkenstock sandals, a coral snake (yes, the red, black and yellow poisonous snakes) slithered on the ground right between my feet! My natural rhythm allowed me to step over it, but heart pounding I really began questioning what I was doing here. I prided myself on going with the flow, but I didn't even know where I was! Maybe I had taken this too far, I thought. I asked myself what if something *had* happened to me with Armando, or what if I had got bitten by the coral snake?

When we got to the bus stop, I was nearly in tears telling Armando I had no idea where I was. He was very sweet and reassuring, telling me to get out my large paper map, and he showed me where we were adjacent to a national park, repeating the names of the towns I needed to know in order to make my way back to Quito. We rode the first bus together, and I paid for his fare as my guide but then we separated, and I paid for his next bus back towards the coast. I now felt confident that indoor plumbing and a good night's sleep would do wonders for my stomach, way more than herbal tea.

I arrived back in Quito just in time to locate a comfortable room for Debra and I in order to communicate with her where to meet me in the city "center" sparing her the uncertainty that I had experienced before. I found something adjacent to the beautiful San Francisco church and plaza. Debra got in late and wanted a glass of wine (per usual), so we ventured out only to remember that it was Good Friday and everything was closed. Everything except for the spectacular colonial church which spans an entire city block that was completely lit up with hymns blasting through the open doors as people lined up on the large staircase for midnight mass. It was so impressive that it was definitely a fair trade off (for me at least) for the lack of wine available. I asked Debra if she wanted to get in line for communion, suggesting the church may have wine. She rejected this idea, but together we laughed and chattered, catching up with one another as we walked the streets back to our hotel.

Spending time with Debra felt way better than I would have ever imagined. Sure, I had met lots of people and other artisan/hippie types along my journey but traveling with Debra made me realize how lonely I was actually becoming. In the past, I had felt called to ramble on, just like the Led Zeppelin lyrics, continuing to travel aimlessly for months or even *years*.[7] Now being with an old friend who I shared a history, language, and culture with was fun and *easy*, and it just felt

[7] Led Zeppelin, "Ramble On," Track #7 on *Led Zeppelin II*, Atlantic, 1969, vinyl

good to have someone to talk and laugh with on the bus. Traveling with Debra made me realize just how challenging it had been to be sick here alone (now twice), and that I still had not found what I had envisioned for myself. I was beginning to feel like this trip was really lacking purpose without having work or a meaningful project to collaborate on.

When we arrived in Otavalo, we oohed and aahed together over the sweaters, though I was mortified when she took a lighter out of her purse and lit some of the fuzz of the wool on fire to see if they were truly alpaca or acrylic. "Put that away," I begged, but she brushed me off saying that if it was alpaca like they claimed it was, it wouldn't do anything.

"Acrylic would melt," she told me unphased, lighting another garment on fire as I buried my eyes in my hands unable to watch.

We picked out a few sweaters, but she decided they were too bulky to haul back. Instead, she honed in on some beautiful but heavy stainless-steel jewelry, scarves, and the leather town of Cotacachi that she wanted to visit. We managed to fill six new large leather bags quite quickly with luggage, wallets, belts, purses and more. After just two days, she had no more space or money to spend, so we headed back to Quito to store her bags before traveling a few more days together. Still not very familiar with Quito, we went door to door to a few random cheap hotels in the same shady part of town where I had been staying until one finally agreed to hold Debra's bags while we went to the hot springs in Baños. We promised that we would stay at the hotel upon our return.

It was a weekend, so the hot springs now felt more like a public pool than my weekday experience, something that hadn't occurred to me, but we made the best of it. We talked, laughed and relaxed as well as engaged in conversation with the families and children playing all around us. We popped in to say hello to Alma while we were there, and I inquired about volunteering with her orphanage project once again to see if this couldn't be the thing to bring a little more meaning and direction into my new life abroad. This time my request was met with a solid maybe.

When we returned to Quito (always guzzling water to prepare for the 10,000-foot altitude), Debra was confident there had to be a more touristic area of the city and asked at the hotel. Sure enough, we found Avenida Amazonas which was sprinkled with cool hostels and international restaurants. We ate dinner there but returned to our dingy hotel we had already committed to stay at. Now that I knew about this area, I had to admit that it was nice to be in a more international zone where I felt safer and less alone. I told myself that from then on I would stay there whenever I was in Quito. No more "Central Hotels" for me.

Debra had to get up super early to make her flight the following day. As I walked her out to the taxi and we exchanged hugs and goodbyes, I was already missing having a travel companion. Her leaving was making me realize I was tired of traveling on my own. All together having been in Puerto Rico and Costa Rica prior to this, it had been over five months now, the longest solo trip I had ever done. Seeing Debra made me miss friends back home and made me realize I wished I had a partner or someone that I could continue to share this journey with. I went back to bed not knowing where I would go next and feeling less than motivated to go back to bussing on my own.

Later that day, I switched my home base to Amazonas Avenue and spent some time researching other places in South America that had been on my bucket list; mainly Machu Picchu, Peru and Brazil. It was an eighteen-hour bus ride just to the border of Peru. Machu Picchu was *days* of bus rides away, as was Brazil, and I no longer had enough money to fly. I wondered if I shouldn't go back to Costa Rica since I knew I had work in Puerto Viejo, and it did feel like it could be "my place." The nearby beach there, Punta Uva, was probably the most beautiful beach I had ever been to. I could absolutely imagine myself living inland from there amongst the lush tropical jungle, toucans, sloths, and monkeys. Though if I used my credit card for that plane ticket, I ran the risk of not having enough money to get back to Alaska where I had the most income potential, great friends like Debra, and all my possessions stored. I checked my e-mail to see if cute California dude had responded. Maybe we could meet back up in Puerto Viejo as well I thought, but *nothing*. With my budget getting extremely tight, I knew if I was going to see more of South America I would need to get moving. I slept on it instead.

Chapter 4

Corrupting the Hare Krishnas

The thought of traveling such long distances alone on buses, especially with all of the machismo, was no longer appealing. And now with my funds becoming alarmingly low, I was reconciling with the fact that I was probably *not* going to be traversing the entire region of South America. Not yet at least. I needed some work or a volunteer position that would help me save money, otherwise I would probably have to return to my home base in Kodiak, Alaska. I had lots of regular massage clients there, and in the past after traveling for a few months, I was always able to build my clientele back up again. Though, that was my plan b. I had really hoped to branch out on this trip; to experience other places and possibly other opportunities which would allow me to be of service in a different way. I thought about Alma's orphanage project again. This was exactly the sort of thing I had envisioned, and who knows, maybe it could somehow turn into a paid position someday. I decided to go back to Baños one last time to ask her about volunteering, and if that didn't work out, maybe something else would present itself. If not, I needed to consider returning to Alaska.

Upon yet another return to Alma's home, she confessed that she admired my tenacity but really wasn't at the volunteer stage yet, as there were still no children or even a finished structure for the orphanage. She said she would speak to the architect to see if I could be of service to him, but after attempting his number a few times, she told me to check back in with her later because the project was forty minutes east of Baños and there was limited communications in that area. She also mentioned the only thing near the building site was a Hare Krishna farm where her architect had been living and eating and that she would need to speak to the Krishnas to see if they could also provide my room and board. I had just assumed the project was in Baños, so this added substantially more adventure, culture, and now even religion to the only volunteer breadcrumbs I had really seen on this journey.

Alma had spoken to Martín the architect and they agreed to let me stay for a one-week trial period to see if I could help him with any of the preliminary work for the project. I didn't know what that meant, but later that day, I was excited to be heading to the Hare Krishna farm and followed instructions to get off the bus in Rio Negro. Surrounded by nothing but trees and countryside, I walked a few kilometers down a dirt road before I saw a wooden sign pointing the way to Govinda's Eco Lodge & Restaurant. My destination had only been described as the *finca* (or farm) of the Hare Krishnas but with the name Govinda and the lotus flower on the sign, I assumed this was the place. I was welcomed warmly by several volunteers and two young German men who were devotees, named Vijay and Prasad.

They immediately began to familiarize me with their daily happenings (including temple every morning) and invited me to prayer at 4:30 a.m. I was looking forward to taking part in *something* while I was there, but I hadn't imagined it would be at that hour. Apparently, I didn't do a very good job at hiding my shock at such an early schedule because as Prasad helped me with my backpack and showed me to my room, my outward hesitation gave way to a deeper discussion. As Prasad and I sat cross legged in front of one another on the wooden planks of the floor in my simple room, he asked how familiar I was with the Krishna faith. I admitted that my knowledge base was limited to seeing groups chanting inside the airport, orange robes, shaven heads, and tambourines. "I do have a friend who grew up on a Krishna farm though," I rattled on, telling him the most senseless details I knew. "They sold incense and gave books away, one of which I received and had begun reading, but never finished, the Bhagavad Gita."

Surprisingly, Prasad lit up, not as a result of what I considered my ignorance, but with the mention of the Bhagavad Gita. This is their most sacred text he explained, and as such, it confirmed that I was further along on the path than I had originally thought.

I'm somewhat ashamed to admit that as someone who is highly interested in spirituality, I've read lots of spiritual texts *part way through*: *The Tibetan Book of the Dead*, *Tao Te Ching*, and *The Yoga Sutras* amongst many others. I love Eastern Philosophy and I really wish I *could* read an entire book of sacred text, but the language is really difficult for me. Often times, I feel like I need to be able to truly understand or embody what I read before I move on. But just like the bible, I could focus on assimilating one verse my whole life. So, what happens is I read something like, "You have a right to perform your prescribed duties, but you are not entitled to the fruits of your actions. Never consider yourself to be the cause of the results of your activities, nor be attached to inaction," in the Bhagavad Gita and think dammmnnnnn, that's a hard one, close the book, and never pick it up again.[8] I've also come to realize that I'm an experiential learner. This is probably another reason why I became so addicted to travel because I learn best through doing, having new experiences, and conversations such as these.

Prasad was clearly happy to share more. He began to divulge *why* they begin chanting mantras at 4:30 a.m. "The early morning hours are when our bodies are most vulnerable to being possessed by ill-intended spirits. Those who do not live a spiritual life are at greater risk of this," he explained. "These spirits or *Jinns* seek earthly pleasures, such as wealth, food, sex, drugs…" *rock n' roll maybe*, I interjected in my mind, imagining myself at many an amazing concert partaking in nearly all of those things. "They are able to possess those who are weak in character and then live vicariously through them, overindulging at the unsuspecting humans' expense. The Hare Krishna vow of celibacy, vegetarianism, commitment to chanting and meditation all serve to enrich our spiritual lives as well as protect against evil spirits."

Having never heard this reason given for avoiding substances and certain behaviors, I became very curious about this, especially because I could obviously be at risk. I did know that Krishnaism had originated before Christianity, so in my mind, surely such a longstanding faith *did* have some validity. In an attempt to learn more, and also in my own

[8] Bhagavad Gita: Chapter 2, Verse 47

defense, I offered that I was vegetarian, currently vegan-vegetarian (*plus, plus, no?*) and practiced semi-regular meditation. "Mmmmm," he said shaking his head in disapproval, "Spiritual dedication goes beyond just diet. I realize now how lost I was when I was using alcohol and drugs, as if those substances or something else entirely was controlling me. Krishnaism provided so many answers and such a positive direction for me at a time in my life when I needed it most."

Hmmmm, I thought, respecting his beliefs and opinions. But as a marijuana and psychedelic advocate, I knew we would just have to agree to disagree on that one. He was only twenty-four years old, so I asked how his family felt about his subscribing to this belief system, fully aware that most people, especially parents, assume the Krishna faith is a cult. Prasad shared that his family has been very supportive saying that he had always been a seeker, unlike Vijay's parents whose outward disapproval had led to a communication breakdown.

Highly animated now, he shared more testimony explaining how their Swami, who is from India but now lives in the Krishna Center in Baños, had given them their Hindu names. "When 'Swami' (I began to notice he always referred to him this way) was younger, he had been living a life of abundance on the material plane with no spiritual sustenance. In fact, it was during an accident in his red convertible sports car that he had a spiritual awakening as his many past lives were shown to him passing as fleeting images in his brain while he was unconscious. This incident led him back to his Hindu faith, and eventually one specific branch of Hinduism, Krishnaism. He renounced all of his worldly possessions letting go of desire which was a symbol of his faith in the divine, and his faith that Lord Krishna would provide for his needs. He vowed to devote all of his efforts to cultivating spiritual realization and to the service of others on the same path." Prasad was clearly moved by the power of this story and the serious commitment Swami had made. And I felt something within me lighting up as well. Swami's near-death experience, although different from mine, served to reinforce what I had come to believe about NDEs *and* psychedelics which is that these experiences have the potential (amongst many other benefits and capabilities) to magnify the images that we hold in our subconscious minds. Swami had grown up in India where reincarnation was the dominating belief, whereas the afterlife that I saw was more angelic and a representation of the Christian and counterculture influence in my life. I could also relate to wanting to renounce my worldly possessions. In fact, I had on a certain level when I was younger, but that was not seen as an act of faith or devotion at all. In American culture, that's deemed as irresponsible and undesirable. I thought about the fact that in Eastern cultures Swamis, Indian Sadhus (or holy men), and Buddhist monks who beg for alms are more understood and often revered.

Prasad interrupted my thoughts by asking if I believed in reincarnation. "Well… yes," I replied hesitantly. "I *do* believe in reincarnation, but I haven't been shown any direct evidence of it in my own life. At least not yet, not like Swami."

This reminded me that I had *just* been asking myself questions regarding karma and reincarnation as it related to the possible bus accident. I acknowledged how amazing it was that I was now having a conversation about that exact thing with a Hare Krishna devotee in such an unexpected environment (*I mean, Hare Krishnas in Ecuador!?*) where I now had the opportunity to learn more first-hand.

"Do you practice yoga?" Prasad asked, becoming physically bouncy when I responded yes. He wanted to know if I could teach them yoga while I was there explaining that their vision for the center was to offer regular yoga classes as an activity that appealed to the general public to hopefully attract more visitors. I liked to show my massage clients stretches they could do to help relieve their chronic pain, and I had attended yoga classes regularly in Kodiak. But I wasn't comfortable leading a complete yoga class, so instead I offered to teach them some basic massage techniques which could also be a service they offered to guests. Beaming, he said he would share this good news with Swami and see when we could get started on this side volunteer project. Before excusing himself to help with dinner preparations he invited me to temple once more the following day at yes, 4:30 a.m. It hadn't changed.

Satisfied with having been led here, as well as another project having surfaced for me, I began to hum while I unpacked a bit. Aretha Franklin's, "The moment I wake up, before I put on my makeup, I say a little prayer for you," came through. Though I still doubted that four in the morning would be the moment I would wake up.[9]

Before dinner, I went to meet the Spanish architect Martín and see what my first volunteer week would look like. He welcomed me into his small private cabaña where he was staying, between the road and a rushing creek, and began to show me the plans for the project. I wasn't familiar with reading architectural plans at that time, but it looked quite involved with one large central building and a few other smaller structures which would serve as staff housing. Martín

[9] Song originally recorded by Dionne Warwick, "I Say a Little Prayer," side A of single *The Windows of The World*, Scepter, 1967, vinyl

alternated between Spanish and English, sometimes losing me, but I did my best to follow his eccentric hand gestures and general disapproval. From what I could tell, he was ranting about not receiving any help and the lack of funding for the project. As we walked to the site, he began grumbling about the Krishna's vegetarian food not knowing I was a vegetarian. When I revealed that I too was vegetarian he added, "They're nice people. I'm just tired of tofu, rice and lentils."

When we arrived at the building site, I was definitely able to identify with his frustration as there was absolutely nothing started. Just a large overgrown parcel of land. This led to more grumbling about how he needed a crew to begin leveling the land, measuring, and stringing off where the actual buildings would be constructed. "It looks as if you and I are the crew for now," he said, and although he seemed extremely doubtful, we made plans to meet with shovels the following morning.

Everyone in the kitchen was accommodating with my vegan (and now gluten-free to see if that would help my continuing stomach issue) dietary needs. We talked and shared throughout the meal, and it was agreed that once we had Swami's blessing, massage courses would be held in the afternoons after my excavation work at the orphanage site. It felt good being here, and I went to bed happy to have finally found some purpose. Though I have to admit, that I did have visions of floating demon spirits who could possibly take over my body while I was sleeping. Later, when I was spooked by the floorboards creaking in the dark, I knew the most logical explanation was that early morning had arrived and the others were tip-toeing off to temple. I rolled over guilt free and enjoyed two more hours of blissful, demon-less sleep. When I awoke, I was excited to see what would unfold during my first full day.

After breakfast I went to Martín's cabaña where I found him finishing his coffee, spam, and eggs, clearly taking breakfast matters into his own hands. We exchanged pleasantries as he gathered a few metal stakes, a large measuring tape, a pickax, and a shovel. As we walked by the beautiful blue Krishna fountain set alongside of the road, Martín pointed out the temple asking if they had converted me yet. "No," I replied and shared that I hadn't attended this morning. He warned me against such ludicrous beliefs and hours, but I didn't see any actual risk in praying.

Once at the site Martín decided the best tactic was to clear the overgrown grass and create a footpath that circumnavigated the entire property. I set about removing large clumps of grass by the roots with my shovel where the trail would be. It was slow going, hot and humid, but I thought it was doable, at least on level ground. It proved to be more complicated pretty early on as I worked on a gentle slope, thinking to cut stairs in as I went up. Just below the soil was metamorphic rock, a result of the nearby active Tungurahue Volcano. I called Martín over as I wedged the shovel beneath a large flat stone. "Errrrgghhhh," I groaned as I tried to use my body weight as a lever to raise it. This produced more distress, and he began shouting, "I am an architect, not a geologist or a field worker! This is *absolutamente loco* that I am out here working with a shovel in the dirt! I am only doing it because, you, you, you, they send me YOU, a little American girl to work!" He shook his head in disbelief.

I completely understood him and said I was only trying to help, offering the suggestion that we use the stones as stairs. He apologized, saying he wasn't mad at me. He was just frustrated that he had been staying there a month and was yet to receive any money or workers to begin the project. He also communicated that he knew Alma was doing her best to raise funds in Germany, and hopefully when she returned from a meeting in Quito, we would know more. This week would be a decision maker or breaker for him because he couldn't continue to live there, now paying for his own canned meat, without more funding. I didn't take any of this personally, and we agreed to finish that section of the slope, digging out the stones together to use them as stairs. Then we headed back for lunch.

After lunch it began to pour down rain. I borrowed an umbrella and went to check on Martín who confirmed there would be no more work for the day. Vijay had spoken to Swami on the phone about the possibility of beginning basic massage lessons. Swami had expressed his concern that touch and massage are quite sensual. His fear was that this intimacy could create unnecessary temptation as both devotees had been celibate for over a year. My idea had been to alternate training Prasad and Vijay, talking them through while they practiced on one another. I saw no harm in that, and Swami hadn't openly objected, so we began.

The following morning (still no temple for me), Martín and I set off to work again. When we arrived at the site, we saw that the rain had washed out our stairs, displacing the rocks and leaving our trail a muddy mess. I would need rain boots to continue, and Martín would need an entirely new attitude. He was done. He would wait to see if Alma would be able to fund a real crew for him any time soon. So, even though the orphanage didn't look like it was going to hold much future for me, I was happy to dive in a bit deeper with the Hare Krishnas, to practice yoga, hike, and continue with my mini massage course.

About day three of the massage training, Swami arrived. Just as we had been doing, Prasad was practicing on Vijay, and I was training him to fine tune his senses to look for tension in the body. Swami stood over all of us working on yoga mats, shaking his head and said he still disapproved. Prasad jumped up to have a conversation with him explaining that they had only been working on one another and that he and Vijay were like brothers. Swami expressed that his concern was not only if they were to provide massages to women at the center in the future, but also that after years of celibacy, temptation can come in many forms, even touching another brother of the same faith. Prasad agreed but asked if they could continue the training while I was still there just a few more days. They wanted to have the knowledge that they could later pass on to other residents and maybe non-devotees to provide massage services. Swami reluctantly agreed, sighing and walking away.

In all honesty, if the subject of sensuality and the possible temptation of massage wasn't brought up, this would have never occurred to me. As a professional therapist, I had received training in ethics and confidentiality, which I held in high esteem. I had always viewed my treatments as strictly therapeutic. In fact, as a licensed therapist, I felt I had a duty to help reverse the stigmatization of massage having a sexual connotation. But after that visit from Swami, I began to think just how erotic it would be if those two *were* somehow corrupted by my massage lessons and what that would mean. I wondered if they would be tempted to touch one another sexually, or to touch me, possibly both of them, at the same time. As I reminded myself that they hadn't felt the touch of a woman in over a year, my rebellious nature agreed with my inner optimist that this type of rule breaking was completely attainable. I did a quick assessment and decided that even though I found the brunette Vijay much more attractive than baby-faced Prasad, he was too cold and distant to even try to pursue. Prasad and I had made a nice connection through our conversations from the very beginning, so he would be the focus of my fantasy. Maybe we should begin by having Prasad practice on me so I can critique his work, I thought. Maybe the sex would be so good it will cause him to rethink the celibacy aspect of his faith? I wasn't proud of this thinking. In fact, I did feel a bit bad, realizing how difficult a year of celibacy probably was for a twenty-four-year-old male, but I shifted the blame onto Swami and the forbidden fruit effect.

May 13th was my 27th birthday, and I decided to make it memorable by pushing myself to go to temple at 4:30 a.m. I stood on a yoga mat and watched as together both devotees and non-devotees recited a whole chain of complicated Sanskrit mantras that were impossible to fake lip sync. Then they began the classic maha-mantra: Hare Krishna Hare Krishna, Krishna Krishna Hare Hare, Hare Rama Hare Rama, Rama Rama Hare Hare. I was able to follow this part, but after counting one round of 108 chants on beads, they did a yogic chaturanga, bowing down in prayer before they started all over again with another unfamiliar prayer and the maha-mantra. I gave up and sat in meditation, as I had been instructed to do any time if I felt lost or uncertain. I sat there absorbing all their devotion as they continued chanting their 16 rounds of 108 chants and 1,728 maha-mantras. Their faith and discipline *were* beautiful. I felt waves of gratitude and shame come in. Gratitude for this experience having found its way into my life, and shame for what was quickly becoming a highly entertaining fantasy; the idea of sexually corrupting Prasad's (and possibly Vijay's) faith. I had chalked this up to just a momentary challenge, but now I wondered if this couldn't somehow become more. Maybe, I thought, after leaving his faith, Prasad would be willing to travel with me.

That night at dinner, in honor of my birthday, the volunteers made a special cheese-less pizza with mashed potato crust and a gluten-free vegan carrot cake. It was so thoughtful and slightly comical that everyone was so eager to try the cake since it was a new addition to their usual meal plan (as Martín had said) of tofu, rice and lentils. They were also buzzing with excitement about Prasad and Vijay's upcoming adventure to the Krishna Center in Baños. As my week was nearly up, and there was still no answer from Alma, it had been decided that I would return to Baños together with the two devotees on the bus. I hadn't had the nerve to suggest Prasad touch me during our last lessons, but this was to be an overnight trip, and I was hopeful I could lead him into temptation to have at least one night together in Baños. My daydream now included one night leading to more time together, possibly traveling, a relationship, or him returning to Kodiak with me, or me going to Germany with him. The Krishna Center in Baños provided free vegetarian meals to the public on Sundays, so we planned on my attending Swami's afternoon service with them and then we would all have dinner together. I would possibly stay the night there, or if things went well, entice Prasad to stay the night with me in a nearby hotel.

The following morning the three of us set out walking on the dirt road to catch the bus. I was determined to sit next to Prasad, my plan being to hold his hand or touch his thigh on the bus ride to make my intentions known. As we walked, the two of them talked excitedly about the opportunity to earn more money for the center in Rio Negro with incense and book sales this trip. Prasad said he had a planned phone call with his parents from Baños that day, and at the mention of this Vijay became visibly stiff, walking ahead of us. Prasad told me that he was purposely open about his relationship with his family in hopes to inspire Vijay to continue trying with his. I remembered the "communication breakdown" he had mentioned before and thought of the Led Zeppelin song with the same title.

As we boarded the bus, I became disappointed as there were not two seats left for us to sit together. I opted for the next best thing; two aisle seats across from one another, motioning for Prasad to sit near me. It wasn't as intimate, but I could still convey my interest reaching across the aisle. To my dismay, he chose to sit diagonally, one row ahead of me in the aisle to be across from Vijay who was seated directly in front of me. *Hmmmph.* They were clearly shining and full of energy. As the bus started moving, they both stood up and made their way to the front. To my horror, Prasad became an annoying traveling bus salesman, the ones I had ignored everywhere on the buses thus far in Ecuador. The people that walk the aisle passing their items for sale to each passenger, allowing them to hold their product while they return to the front of the bus to present their sales pitch. Previously, I had always refused to hold an object that I had no interest in purchasing with the cultural excuse of not understanding the language or the concept. He and Vijay walked along handing out small books and incense to everyone. For the first time, I personally knew the salesmen, so now I clearly understood it would be rude of me not to accept. They asked us in Spanish, "How many of you think you know God? Do you know God is in many forms, but the supreme God is Krishna? Are you interested in learning more about Lord Krishna? Consciousness? Living a healthier lifestyle via a vegetarian diet? Yoga? Meditation? These books hold the answers to the questions you yearn to discover. Everyone on this bus is personally invited to the Krishna Center in Rio Negro or Baños. If you have any questions or would like to take part in vegetarian cooking, in prayer, or in meditation practice come and join us."

We were all urged to purchase the literature or incense in our hands as the proceeds would all go towards their foundation. They thanked everyone for their time, as all good bus salesmen do, and began walking the aisle to collect a few payments for incense as well as the unsold items. I don't know what bothered me more; the fact that Prasad was an annoying bus salesman or the possibility that I wasn't that special because they openly invite busloads of people to come visit and stay with them on the regular. All of my hopes of corruption were dashed with Prasad's obvious focus on his spirituality and the center. There were just too many insurmountable (literally) obstacles between us to move forward in my fantasy relationship. As I handed the small book back, I heard those Led Zeppelin lyrics in my head, "Communication breakdown, it's always the same, I'm having a nervous breakdown, drive me insane… waaahhhhh."[10]

With that turn of events, I could begin to shift my attention towards getting through this last sitting with Swami and onto finding a hotel for the evening. With my money nearly gone and no other volunteer opportunities in sight, I would need an Internet Café to book a flight back to Kodiak, Alaska. As people began to file in for Sunday service, I was pleasantly surprised to see a diverse group in attendance. There were Ecuadorians, Indians, and international residents present. Service included a Kirtan with a few people playing instruments and leading in song, dance, and of course, the maha-mantra. There was a short lecture on spiritual text in Spanish, so I was lost there. And then finally, the Sunday feast that I had heard so much about. As I made my way along the buffet, Prasad was in my ear explaining that Sunday service gave the public an opportunity to experience Krishna consciousness at the center as well as try their yummy food that they normally sell in the restaurant (in that same space) during the week. He added I was welcome to leave a donation as my token of appreciation for the meal. At that point, my feelings for Prasad had taken a 180 degree turn as I was quite done with incense sales and suggested donations.

I gravitated toward another North American woman about my age who had attended service. She and I sat and ate together. She offered that she had been living in Baños the last six months and tried to attend Kirtan on Sundays to get a little more international exposure while out of the house. Plus, she loved their vegetarian

[10] Led Zeppelin, "Communication Breakdown," track #7 on Led Zeppelin, Atlantic, 1969, vinyl

food. We made a comfortable connection with me sharing the more appropriate events of the previous week and the need for the Internet to buy my return plane ticket. With that, she invited me to stay the night, or a few nights if need be, in her spacious apartment where she would help me book my ticket on her computer. Done! We shared a lovely evening together indulging in wine, stories, and laughter. I booked a last-minute plane ticket on my emergency credit card, and I decided to leave the following day and spend two nights in my newly discovered Amazonas area before flying out.

As I set off on the four-hour bus ride, my mind was already in the future formulating a new plan. I envisioned myself landing in Kodiak and attempting to rent my old office space once again. I would arrive broke (in debt actually) and have to begin reestablishing my massage business. I thought about how I loved being in Latin America, but I just hadn't found the right thing that could actually support me living there full time. I wondered if I could just go back to Alaska long enough to save some money in order to *buy* a small parcel of land somewhere down here, possibly in Costa Rica, *on my own?* I had loved being in Puerto Viejo living happy and carefree, peddling a bike to the local market, through the lush jungle, and to beautiful beaches amongst the sloths, monkeys, and toucans. And having worked there doing massage previously, I knew it was possible. I pictured building a simple two-story home that had my massage studio downstairs with a small apartment upstairs for myself. All I needed was a bike for transportation, and I could live well off of just a few massage treatments a week, eating *gallo pinto*, coconuts, and fresh pineapple. This was it! I realized that in the past so many of my relationships had been in hopes of doing something like this with the right someone, but maybe that someone was me! Jimmy was super adventurous but had lacked responsibility. Kelly and I had looked at property in Honduras, but he had wanted to create some sort of hippie commune. That wasn't my thing. I had begged Riley to travel with me and had just spent months checking my email to see what Jake, the cute California surfer dude who was basically just a casual hook-up, was up to. I saw the ridiculousness of my latest fantasy, thinking a Hare Krishna devotee was going to give up his faith and come travel or live with me. As the bus made the steep climb back into Quito, my own vision was finally becoming clear, and I no longer cared if someone else was willing or able to do this with me. I would go it alone. Heart first!

Chapter 5

Sugar Mama

I hit the ground running when I landed on Kodiak Island. Using the last of my emergency credit line, I would see if I could get my old office space back. It was available, but only under certain aesthetic stipulations because it had taken the property manager three coats of paint to cover the relaxing purple gray that had been on the walls. I contacted close friends who were also massage customers to let them know I was back and in need of some assistance. One friend Clay mentioned he would love to gift his wife ten massages if I had some kind of punch card he could buy for her. This gave way to what I considered a brilliant plan. I would sell massage packages within my close circle of friends that included ten massages for $350 (which normally had a value of $600), hoping it would be an offer they couldn't refuse. I only needed to sell two or three of these packages to start paying my bills and get in my office again. Thankfully, this sounded like a hell-of-a-deal to the people I presented the idea to and before long, my plans were being set in motion.

A house and car were secondary or possibly unnecessary. I knew a lot of people on the island, and in the past, I had lived as a perpetual house sitter. I would get a new bike and use that for transportation. Worst-case scenario, I could always sleep on my massage table in my office. There was a bathroom down the hall, just no shower. When I first arrived, I stayed on some of my best friends' couch who lived in the legendary waterfront Jackson's Trailer Park. Shortly after my arrival, Clay asked if I could house and dog sit for him and his wife the majority of the summer which would also include the use of their car. Perfect!

As a fisherman and volunteer firefighter, Clay didn't take housesitting lightly and scheduled a "safety walk through" with me. This was the first time I had ever experienced this as a *professional* house sitter (my only unprofessional moment being the selling LSD/undercover cop incident). He was going to be in and out fishing all summer, and his wife Reece (one of my best friends) was a teacher and had already left with their young son to spend summer vacation with family in California. He showed me where the main breaker box was for the electricity and where the fire extinguisher was located. In addition, he mentioned his buddy "Holms" might be staying there as well, hoping that was okay. He thought that I probably knew him, explaining he was one of the few people who had also attended their simple outdoor wedding ceremony. He went on to describe him; fisherman, surfer, about his age, and married with a kid but going through a separation with his wife. In my mind I pictured a fat guy (fisherman), with a long gray beard (ZZ Top style) in a white "wife beater" (the ribbed kind) tank top and boxer shorts, sitting on their couch, belly out, scratching his crotch. Surfer never registered. Even though Clay was such a great guy that I knew anyone he was good friends with had to be one too, all I could think was no, *not okay*. Going through a separation with a child sounded like drama, and there would be no privacy living in this small creek side cabin together. I let out a thoughtful moan of disapproval which Clay disregarded saying, "He's a really good buddy, so I gotta' help him out if he needs it. And who knows, maybe he won't take me up on the offer."

I set to work inside my storage space, getting access to more than just what I had in my backpack. The day before Clay left, I borrowed a car to go say goodbye and take some things over to their house. Sure enough, Holms was on his couch. But not the fat, ball scratching, bearded fisherman I had conjured up in my head. He was much more surfer looking; clean cut and handsome with short blonde hair, no beard, big blue eyes, and long eyelashes. He was also fully clothed in blue jeans and a custom sweatshirt that read *Holms- Built for Punishment.* I did recognize him and together we recalled a few other occasions when our paths had crossed. Kodiak is a big island in a huge archipelago, but the actual population of the town is about 6,000 people. We had been at another mutual friends' wedding, and we were both at Clay and Reece's house right after their son was born. I had brought my massage chair over to work on Reece and Matthew Holmgren (hence *Holms*) had helped me carry it back to my car when I was finished.

"Ahhhh, that's right. You're the massage girl," Holms said, now putting two and two together. "How much do you charge by the hour?"

"Sixty dollars," I said with a warm smile thinking he was a potential customer.

"Ohhh wowwww, Sugar Mama! Sixty dollars times eight hours a day is four hundred and eighty dollars a day, times thirty days a month… you're making bank!"

I laughed. "It's not exactly like that. I could never give eight hours of massage a day."

He listened intently and then recalculated, arriving at the conclusion that I was still making enough money to qualify me for Sugar Mama status. He then launched right into his current state of affairs, which having already been in a relationship with someone who was divorced and having experienced ex-wife induced emotions firsthand along with two small children, I really wasn't interested on any level. Not in being in another relationship with someone who already had children, and not being roommates with someone going through a divorce. I was thinking, "save the drama for your baby mama" when surprisingly, I heard full optimism coming out of his mouth. He was saying things like, "It's for the best," and "we were complete opposites." He was also definitely amusing. This made me think that we probably could cook a few drama-free meals together in the house ***if*** we were indeed cohabitating, though I preferred to have this small space to myself.

My first few nights there, Holms did stay on the couch. I was busy organizing boxes and moving myself back into my office space during the day, but in the evening, we cooked and ate dinners together. Matt's hyperbolic sense of humor had me in stitches. Just like the Sugar Mama comment, he was continuing to take random jabs at me when we hardly knew one another which I found refreshing and a good reminder to not take myself too seriously. One night, as we talked in the kitchen, he asked how old I was. He was shocked to learn that I had never been married, and I didn't have a serious boyfriend at the moment. He went from flirting and telling me how unbelievable that was because I was, "so attractive, and *seemed* nice and normal," to doing more math (obviously a strong subject for him). Then he told me, "Welp, you only have three years left."

"Three years left until what?" I asked, feeling flattered and a bit flirtatious myself.

"Until you're thirty, and then it's all over. You'll be past your prime, and it will probably be difficult for you to land a husband or to start a family," he said with a twinkle in his turquoise blue eyes. This was so ridiculous and clearly went against what he had just said so I couldn't take any offense. I burst out laughing, dismissing this completely and saying it was so far from the truth that it wasn't worth discussing. Then, I asked how old he was. When he told me he was thirty-six, I poked right back at him telling him that he wasn't, "that old yet" and shared the fact that I had a ten-year rule in place for myself. I gave him an abbreviated version of my dating history which mostly included men who were much older than me (usually by fifteen years) and therefore in much different phases in their lives. I finished with, "This led to my taking a personal oath to no longer date men more than ten years older than me."

After doing math once again, he pointed out that he was only nine years my senior, which *did* meet my dating criteria. We talked and laughed throughout dinner that night and then danced to his favorite dancehall reggae artists in the living room. I pointed out the fact that since he had brought over all of his CD's he clearly had gone back home, so maybe something had changed and he didn't need to stay on the couch anymore? He admitted that yes, his ex had officially moved out, and he was now free to move back home. I encouraged him to do so because even though he was easy to talk to and getting to know one another felt good, I was determined to stay focused on my goal and not get seriously involved with anyone. I knew I could find a small piece of property in the tropics for eight to ten thousand dollars. I could probably save that in one year's time. After I had the land, I could live there and rent something cheap while I worked to save and build there.

The first day he was on his own, Matt "just so happened" to be slowly walking by my massage office which was on the second floor of a building that hardly had any other businesses upstairs. It was pretty obvious that he had come to see me when he casually peered inside my open door. He blushed and denied that I was the reason he was there but asked, "Since I ran into you, do you need any help with anything?" When he saw the extent of my redecorating, he left to go get his tool box and then returned to help me hang my framed Alaskan art on the walls. He invited me to dinner at his place, saying that he wanted to cook for me to return the favor since I had initiated cooking our meals at the cabin. "Okay, maybe tomorrow," I said, still maintaining my distance. Matt knew my plan was to move to Central America, and once his dissolution of marriage was finalized, he was going back to the suburbs of Chicago where he had grown up. Still, it was undeniable that there was some chemistry between us, and we also had an Alaska-Chicago-California-Florida connection, both of us having lived in or having close family in all of those places. But I needed to start working ASAP, and he was going to start having shared custody of his three-year-old son. I knew we were both about to get really busy in our separate lives. "So .... dinner at my place tomorrow night?" He asked once again. "I can pick you up at the cabin."

"Okay," I agreed. "One dinner."

The dinner at his house led to us spending time together nearly every day; he was helping me get moved back into my office, we went to the beach with his son, and we walked some of my favorite hiking trails. On one occasion, the two of us were out hiking an amazing coastal trail that was remote, on a bluff, and surrounded by wildflowers when we shared our first kiss. Before long, we were in bed together. Matt's pillow talk, as he gently played with my hair, was that he was going to give his truck to me when he left the island. It was a cheap two door, older Toyota pickup which he called, "A beater with a heater," but it ran and was a generous offer. As charming as he was, I was adamant that I would remain emotionally unattached. Days went by, and as we shared more dinners and nights at the cabin, *his* plan began to slowly evolve. *"Or,* we could drive down to Central America together, I drop you off, and you can keep the truck."

I felt honored, but laughed, taking none of this seriously. "That would be nice if you gave me your truck, and it certainly would come in handy, but I don't need it or expect it. We both know Central America is a lonnngggg ways away, distance wise and even time wise. Who knows where either of us will be by then, and I highly doubt your truck would even make it there." I knew Matt had gifted a friend a car in the past, so this wouldn't have been out of character for him. For me, a gift like that was reminiscent of the rainbow spirit. The only time I had heard of someone gifting a car (besides a parent or a spouse) to someone was at the Rainbow Gatherings or Grateful Dead shows where it was rumored that older hippies would just "kick down" a car or a school bus to stoke out a brother or sister in need. So even though Matt's outward appearance wasn't that of a hippie, I saw that he was a hippie at heart, and I liked the fact that like me, he couldn't be put in any one box. Although he wasn't fishing at the time, I knew he was a hard worker, yet was open minded and smoked pot. He had a sense of adventure having studied Spanish in Mexico, worked on a cruise ship, and traveled to Jamaica more than once. However, if he was interested in starting a relationship with me, offering to give me his truck when he left the island wasn't really a building block. It actually evoked the internal question of "when are you leaving" so that I could inherit his truck.

This was the subject matter while we were lying in bed together one morning when I heard Clay in the next room talking on the phone. His boat had docked to deliver fish at the cannery, so he thought to come by the house, see the dog, call his wife, and get a few things. Now this was embarrassing! I came out of the bedroom and sleepily greeted him then went back to completely freak out to Matt. "Oh my God, he couldn't leave us alone for even two weeks!" I was mortified, but the cabin was so small there was no way he wasn't going to notice. Eventually I came out of the back bedroom, and then Holms came out shortly after. Of course Clay noticed. He lit up, and grinning from ear to ear he exclaimed, "*Oh wowwww! Love is in the air!*"

But was it? Even though things were going well between us, I knew that I had finally discovered what I wanted to do, and I was determined not to change my course.

Chapter 6

Transitioning into What

Matt and I had spent nearly a month together and admittedly things felt really good between us. But now that my business was about to officially reopen, and he was going to have primary custody of his son the next six months as part of the unconventional arrangement he and his soon to be ex-wife had both agreed to, I began to prepare him for our inevitable separation. The few times I had seen him with his son Gabriel, I knew he was a very good dad. I noted that he had packed extra undies, pants, socks, and snacks to spend the morning at the beach together. *If* I were to ever be in a relationship with someone who had a child (which was something I was *not* planning on), that was definitely the way it would need to be. The actual parent would need to assume the majority of responsibility, not me, the way I had done in the past. And my partner would need to be unified with me, not his child, thus giving them too much power in our relationship, which was also what I had experienced before. But all of this seemed irrelevant and I told him as much at what was to be our romantic mountain top picnic that turned into a goodbye lunch. We were seated facing one another on a blanket on top of Pillar Mountain, one of the only mountain peaks you can drive to on Kodiak Island. There were insane ocean views, innumerable surrounding islands and mountain peaks in the distance as well as the town and fishing harbor down below. Rather than taking in all of this beauty, he looked into my eyes completely panic stricken. He reached for both of my hands, telling me he thought everything was going so well between us. He said there didn't seem to be a cloud in the sky. We were both happy, healthy individuals completely enjoying one another's company. "Yes," I agreed, "but we knew this was always temporary. Eventually I'm moving to Central America, most likely to Costa Rica, and you're moving back to the Chicago area."

"Michelle," he looked me in the eyes more intently, bringing my hands closer to his heart, "I think we have something really special. I've never felt such a great connection with anyone before."

This was undeniable, and I divulged that *yes*, he did seem to have the best loved traits from my serious exes all rolled into one. "You have a great sense of humor, you're helpful, generous, *open*, sensitive, and *seem* to be supportive!"

"Michelle, I'm telling you, I'm thirty-six years old, and I've never encountered anything like this. I don't think what we have is so easy to find. I really love you," he told me. "Let's not throw this away just yet."

"I love you, too," I replied hesitantly. Not because it wasn't true, but because I knew I should be careful to not fall *in love* with him if going our separate ways was inevitable. I couldn't see how he was going to fit into the goal I had set for myself, or how I was going to fit into his new reality of being a recently divorced single parent moving to the suburbs of Chicago. Even though Matt was an amazing human, and I did love him, I was reluctant to invest too much of my heart into a relationship that I just couldn't see working out.

"What if once I get settled down South, we meet one another in Chicago during Thanksgiving? You've been going there every year anyway to see your family. Or maybe we could go to my parent's place in Florida for the holidays, and then I drive you to Costa Rica and drop you off?"

"Not likely," I told him. "I will need more time to save." I knew that he was right. Everything was going extremely well, but I needed to remain focused on saving to relocate. I couldn't see myself living on Kodiak Island forever, and I was not interested in moving to the Midwest. I began working full time again and saw slightly less of Matt and Gabe, getting together every few days or so.

Once my house and car sitting gig at Clay's was up, Matt bought me a bicycle and made me a sweet card that he taped to the handlebars which read, "To: Michelle, Thank you for all that you do for us, We Love You: Matt and Gabe." Gabe was adorable. He had Matt's huge turquoise blue eyes and long lashes combined with his mom's brunette hair, olive skin, wide smile, and her button nose. It was easy to love Gabe and want to spend time with him as well. We were silly together, and I was always doing something educational with him in a really fun way. But I still wanted to maintain a healthy amount of space so that

Matt could continue to be the parent. I began to bounce around between various housesitting gigs, only staying at his place when I didn't have one of my own. Autumn was setting in, and Matt was still living on Kodiak Island with no plans to move in sight. Instead, he was starting to go out fishing again and was now talking about traveling to Chicago for Thanksgiving *together*.

With winter nearly upon us and his lease about to be up, he was getting serious about going to the 'lower forty-eight' (what Alaskans call the lower forty-eight states) just for a visit at Thanksgiving time to possibly meet one another's families. His idea was to not renew his lease, but instead move out, so that when we returned, we could officially move into a place of our own together with a fresh start. "You can't continue to housesit and stay in your office through winter," he said genuinely concerned.

"Well, I probably could," I responded, never liking to admit defeat or feel as if I have to succumb to the system. I knew that where there is a will, there's a way.

"Okay, yes, you probably could, but wouldn't it simplify things and actually be nice to live together?"

It would be nice to live together, I thought, but I was afraid of getting too comfortable, becoming too attached to both Matt and Gabe, not continuing to save, or letting go of my dream. "I'm still moving to Central America you know," I told him.

At the same time, I knew he was right. Being unhoused, especially in Alaska in the winter, was difficult. "I want to continue to be able to save."

"I know, and if we live together, you can save more money than paying rent on your own. I need a two bedroom so that Gabe can have his own room, so I'll pay two-thirds of the rent."

I knew having a reliable place to live *would* simplify my life but was hesitant to take on too much of a mom role for my own protection and Gabe's as well. I didn't want to become an important aspect of his life and then disappear. The idea of a *new* place together was interesting. I hadn't thought it bothered me, but when I considered living somewhere else without any prior ex-wife history, it did sound much better than moving into his current place. As I continued to feel into this decision, it felt a lot lighter than having to continuously line up new housesitting gigs or sleeping on my massage table. Our love felt good, and this felt right. So, I agreed, which came with an unexpected sense of relief.

We flew into the Chicago area on separate timelines just before Thanksgiving. Me, with a reasonable amount of notice to continue to save money, and Matt and Gabe on last minute tickets because his fishing schedule was unpredictable, depended completely on industry openings and closings, and the elements themselves. We met one another's family after Thanksgiving. He met my aunt, uncle, and young cousin, and I met his parents, brother, sister in-law, and their three daughters. And then, like he had originally talked about, Matt and Gabe drove me all the way to Florida in his mother's car to meet my parents and sister and essentially drop me off to spend Christmas with my family. Gabe was an excellent and adorable little traveler. We all enjoyed road trip games, singing along to music, joking, and each other's company the whole way. Matt's parents had a condo in Florida two hours north of my parents' house where we stayed a few nights before continuing on south of Miami to where my parents lived. Once at my parents, Gabe received lots of love and attention from my family. His presence helped the visit go surprisingly well.

Throughout my youth, I hadn't just chosen a path that was less traveled. I had completely strayed off the path into nomad's land. My life lacked any resemblance to what my normal midwestern parents could have reasonably envisioned for me, shattering their expectations (whether they realized it or not). This caused much more than a communication breakdown; more like a relationship meltdown. However, with a little more time, space, and normalcy on my part, things seemed to be steadily improving. It helped that Matt was probably the most "normal" boyfriend (if that's what he was) I had ever had. His midwestern upbringing paralleled their background of growing up in Michigan where my sister and I were born. Having been raised in Rancho Cucamonga, California (well, technically Alta Loma, but I love the name and the Grateful Dead reference to the song "Pride of Cucamonga"), forty miles east of Los Angeles, I was exposed to and had adopted a more green/progressive mentality. Matt had lived in Huntington Beach for four years, not far from where I grew up, hence our California connection. He had a full spectrum of interests and life experiences, and he really shined. He was happy to talk to my parents about anything; from sports and cars with my dad, to cooking and art with my mom which I could tell they genuinely appreciated.

Matt and Gabe spent a few nights at my parents' house. We all went to Santa's Enchanted Forest as well as to the nearby nature parks. My sister came over, and we all decorated the Christmas tree together. It was easy, wholesome, and happy. Everyone seemed to be hitting it off. Less than a week before Christmas, Matt and Gabe drove all the way back up to Chicago to spend the holidays with the Holms, providing evidence that driving me to Central America wasn't completely out of the question.

Even though my parents outwardly approved of Matt and his son, I hadn't told them I was planning on moving in with them or to Central America for that matter. It wasn't that I was afraid of their reaction, it was that I knew what it would be, and it made no sense to tell them until it was 100% certain. We viewed life so differently that historically I rarely (if ever) asked their opinion about my life's choices because I knew what their reaction would be. In the past, whatever I was considering doing (quitting university, traveling, selling weed) they would have strongly advised me against, so I usually moved forward informing them about my decisions after they were made (or not at all in the case of selling weed). My parents came from a world where you got married before you moved in together, but I had already dashed that hope for them many boyfriends ago. Their traditional mindset was that you saved to purchase a house together in the continental United States of America after said marriage. Even though they had come to Puerto Viejo, Costa Rica to visit me, I doubted they would understand the less-is-more philosophy of actually moving there and living the basic lifestyle I had envisioned for myself. So, I would wait to break that news to them as it came closer on the horizon.

Our plan was to start looking for a place together once Matt and I were both back to Kodiak, but he arrived first and got a head start right after the new year. He called my parent's house to tell me there was a new ocean view duplex available right across the street from what was referred to as Junk Beach. He knew this was my happy place. In my free time I loved to go hiking or beachcombing for treasures to use in mosaic art. He had been there, just poking around looking in the windows, but had an appointment to look at it later. It was a very new two bedroom, with an ocean view, and the price was right. He asked if it looked good, should he just get it? I was pretty excited about the Junk Beach location. Not only that, but it was close enough to downtown that I could ride my bike to work. I trusted his judgment, so I agreed, sight unseen. Riding the high of what seemed like an incredible opportunity, I shared this with my parents who met the news with shrugging and said, "If that's what you want to do Michelle." They also pointed out the fact that Matt has a son, and we hadn't known one another for that long.

When I got back, Matt had already moved us in, and it was nice to be living in a comfortable, new space for the first time in a long while. For years I had rented a cabin in Kodiak right on the beach with a lake in the backyard, but it was fifty years old, funky, and would get quite cold in the winter. This felt like ours, and though nothing had ever been formally discussed, I knew Matt was now researching property in Central America on his laptop. Yes, he had a laptop and a cell phone, but I was still living in the dark ages going to the public library to check my email once or twice a week and to borrow CDs and books. After Matt had worked on a cruise ship (when he was twenty), he had entertained the idea of buying property and living in the tropics, so this was not a novel idea for him. In fact, he had more insight as to where to look for property from the comfort of our own home (on websites and in printed publications) which I would have never thought to do. He found a few interesting things on the islands of Bocas del Toro in Panamá and on the Osa Peninsula located on the Pacific side of Costa Rica that he wanted me to see. I looked over his shoulder at prices and locations but didn't say a whole lot. It was unclear if he was looking *for me* or if he was considering doing this *with me*, and I didn't ask. I was still holding onto the idea of living in Puerto Viejo and moving there on my own.

Regardless of where his future would lead him, we were both on a short-term savings plan now, so we weren't about to invest in furniture. Instead, we made our own with upcycled second hand items or using driftwood and large findings from Mission (or Junk) Beach, which sadly had been a dump site during World War II and for some time after that. This (along with other areas including a HAARP weather control project and a rocket launch site) has raised a lot of questions about health, pollution, and safety on Kodiak Island. People would sometimes joke about HAARP, asking if the military could change the weather, why weren't they doing so because Kodiak is infamous for being rainy and foggy with a climate similar to Seattle. Back in the 1940's, Mission Beach was quite far out of town, but the town has since sprawled way beyond this site. After the war, the military literally left everything there; tanks, forklifts, and even airplane parts amongst other waste. Years later, the dump was officially moved inland, but this area of the coast was never cleaned up.

Every time I crossed the asphalt road in front of our house and made my way down the steep twenty-foot cliff, all of this would be a sort of mind-blowing irony. First, the contrast between the incredible natural beauty of this area against the large rusty heavy machinery parts scattered on the beach was striking. Spruce trees were growing up out of old abandoned military vehicles. A closer look would reveal toilets, car parts, pieces of antique dishes, old keys, beach glass, reflectors, bike chains, peddles, marbles, emblems, and so much more. All in one of the most pristine settings you could imagine, on a remote island in the middle of the Gulf of Alaska. The cold winter air would swirl all around me as waves crashed and eagles flew overhead. The irony of all of this was that I knew it was so wrong, but admittedly, this was my guilty pleasure. I would get super excited about the possibilities of what I could find here. We all did, actually, and this became one of our favorite pastimes together. We hauled back small buckets of driftwood, tumbled ceramics, and beach glass (including blues and the coveted reds and yellows). We had a "things with holes in them" collection amongst what we called our "treasures." When we would get home, we would pour everything out on cardboard on the kitchen floor for it to dry and Gabe (now staying with us every other weekend) would spend hours sorting treasures by color or category. It was the perfect three-year-old activity and he loved it. So much so, that one day when he first arrived for the weekend, he asked me in his adorable little still-learning-to-talk voice, "You know what I'm thinkin'?" Which no, I did not. "I'm thinkin' it's pro-lly low tide," he informed me, basically letting me know exactly what he wanted to do, as we could only go beachcombing at low tide. I was thoroughly impressed with this little artistic connected-to-the-sea nature boy. Together we repurposed our treasures making mosaic vases, picture frames, tables, masks, and stringing things with holes in them into what I called "junk ladders."

Part of what had drawn me to Alaska was its ruggedness, its extremeness, and it being about as far away from an "ordinary" life as possible in the US of A. Living with and being in a relationship with an Alaskan fisherman was anything but ordinary. Matt would be out fishing (and I wouldn't see or hear from him) for days, sometimes a week at a time. When we first moved in together, I didn't care what time of day (or night) they came into port to deliver their fish; I wanted to see him. Matt would call me at all hours of the night, and I'd drive (now sharing his little beater truck) down to the docks to pick him up. At times, he'd just show up having received a ride from his captain or a friend and strip down leaving his fishy clothes on the front porch. Then he would shower and surprise me in bed. I loved this and admittedly, it was becoming quite comfortable; the sex, the snuggling, and the catching up for hours after not seeing one another for days.

A few months in, they were planning a trip out west to Dutch Harbor to fish for halibut. This was over 800 miles away, and they would stay out until they caught their quota, some 70,000 pounds. For the first time, he would be gone for weeks including Easter, so I went down to the dock to say goodbye to everyone. The captain's wife had brought them a casserole and dessert to take with them and to me it felt like the hands of time had rolled back a few hundred years. She was dressed in a long flowing dress, nice shoes, and a warm winter coat, and it just seemed so old fashioned. The women were bringing food down to the waterside to see the men off on their arduous journey during which I would have no contact with them. There was a satellite phone on the boat for emergencies or for the captain to call his wife, but if I wanted to know if they were okay, I'd have to phone her. These were dangerously rough and frigid seas which only reiterated that this was a lifestyle that I could not imagine long-term for either one of us.

Kodiak is primarily a fishing community and because of that and its proximity to Russia and Japan, it has a large Coast Guard base there as well. As I putzed around the house cleaning or working on projects I would listen to the radio. In between music and programs, the marine weather forecast would air. It would not be uncommon to hear phrases like, "Heavy Freezing Spray Warning, Small Craft Advisory, Seas to 35 Feet, Winds Increasing to 50 Knots." I'd listen to the broadcaster rattle off a list of locations (Area 3A, Area 3B, Shelikof Strait) for the small craft advisory, and if Matt's area was named, I would hope that they were able to anchor somewhere safely for the night.

Matt had been fishing around Dutch Harbor for over two weeks before I finally heard from him directly, and their plans had changed dramatically. They had been delayed due to the orca whale activity where they were fishing. He said that every time they ran the hydraulics on the boat, especially to haul in their gear, it was like a dinner bell for the orca whales. They would circle up and feast on the halibut, only leaving lips and heads on the hooks. It took days of *not* fishing for the whales to move on, and now they were finally nearing their quota. Matt told me that the price for halibut per pound was so much higher in Bellingham, Washington, and it was worth it for them to deliver there instead. That would mean a bigger paycheck but more time away. The boat would stay in Washington State so Matt would have to fly home, *or* he suggested that I fly there to meet him. He had an Alaskan Airlines credit card which had an annual promotion of a companion fare where friends fly for $99. He asked me to look into how far south this could get us to see if we could go to Mexico or Central America for a quick vacation and to look at property before he had six months of primary custody of Gabe again. This sounded fun but not in alignment with my current savings plan, so I declined, still keeping my eyes on the prize. "Just see how much it would be," he encouraged me, saying he would pay for the trip. As he was in transit, I was on the phone with Alaskan Airlines (that's how you bought airline tickets back then, that or a travel agent) and had learned that he could fly as far south as Cancun, Mexico for $399 roundtrip from Seattle. My ticket would be an addition $99. Then, I thought we could travel the short distance by land into Belize. I didn't hear from him for days, but when I finally did, he was game. He liked the idea of looking at property in Belize and pointed out this would be a good opportunity to see if we travel well together internationally, which I hadn't really even considered. The more I thought about it, the more I realized this would be a great way to test the waters of building some sort of future together abroad. Things *were* going swimmingly between all three of us, but I didn't know if we would be on the same page when it came to destinations, property, or business ideas. I wasn't sure if relocation was realistic for him when he had the responsibility of being a father. He gave me his credit card number over the phone to purchase the Mexico tickets and told me he trusted me to purchase all the other tickets we needed to get myself to Washington State and him back home to Kodiak. The next time we spoke, I told him I would see him in Seattle in ten days. I began to see this trip as a huge indication as to whether or not we could build a future together, and I was becoming increasingly more curious to see what this first international adventure would determine, if anything.

Chapter 7

When You Know, You Know

Travel had absolutely defined me for *years* following my decision that the *world,* not university, was going to be my teacher (when I was eighteen years old), so it suddenly made sense that traveling *together* could somehow redefine our relationship and/or teach us more about one another and our possible future together. I had always traveled on a shoestring budget, not wanting to continue to save and wait for the perfect moment because I knew that moment or money may never come. Instead, I just got out there and did the damn thing so I could *actually* travel. Being open to adventure had taught me so much about life, the world, and myself that I was curious to see how Matt moved about in the world. Was he a risk taker, too? How inclined was he to planning, and how comfortable was he with just going with the flow and being open to receive life's gifts?

A friend recently told me that according to metaphysical law, there are three ways to learn; either via divine grace, through experiences, or ultimately suffering, and in that exact order. If we don't learn life's lessons through divine grace (which can be divine influence/intervention, blessings, gifts, opportunities, circumstances, etc.), we are shown through experience. And if that is still not getting our attention, then we suffer. We suffer until we are able to incorporate the lesson or change in order to become a better version of ourselves. Looking back, I'm grateful that I have learned mostly through experience and divine grace. At times, the divine gifts that were presented to me were so powerful there was no way *not* to notice and learn from them, even at a young age.

Growing up, my parents had emphasized the importance of hard work, earning money and saving with such an air of absolution, that for me, it was screaming to be challenged. In the fifth grade, when I wanted a ghetto blaster (yes, this is what everyone in my white ten-year-old world called these large battery-operated portable cassette players back then), my mom sat me down so together we could work out the math of just how long it would take me to save my allowance for this $50 ticket item. Undoubtedly, my responsible mother had been looking forward to the moment when she could start to explain the importance of budgeting to me, but I found it completely annoying. For one, I knew they could probably afford to buy it for me if they wanted to. Secondly, it would take me *months* to save up for this, which to a ten-year-old, felt like an eternity. And the only other options that were presented to me were waiting until my birthday or Christmas which were even further away. I loved music, and this couldn't wait. It occurred to me that there had to be another way. A third door.[11] Shortly after our discussion, I went to an orthodontist

[11] The Third Door is a book by Alex Banayan wherein through celebrity interviews he discovers that all of them claim the secret to their success was that they took the third door. They looked for another way in. Alex uses the analogy of a night club. "There's the

appointment where I saw a boombox on display, that of course, got my attention. My line of questioning was interrupted with the orthodontist's instruments in my mouth, but as I laid back in the chair, he told me all that I needed to know. They were raffling off the radio as a prize, and I was welcomed to put my name in the drawing. When I won the boombox a few weeks later, this was quite possibly my first experience with divine grace. This gift woke me up to the idea that there *were* exceptions to the rules of life that I was being presented with and it made me wonder what other obstacles (such as money being the only way to receive something) were just an illusion.

At hippie fests in my teens, I was introduced to barter circles. While traveling, I saw examples of bartering economies where people helped one another to build simple structures or harvest crops in exchange for a communal meal or a share of the harvest. The idea of barter was liberating to me. It was an authentic peer to peer exchange for goods and services that lacked the financial greed of capitalism and sometimes any expectations of payment whatsoever, being more of a gifting economy. This further opened my eyes and gave me the confidence to travel without allowing one illusionary element like my bank account to restrict my potential. I *was* Tom Petty's "American Girl." "She couldn't help thinkin' that there was a little more to life somewhere else, after all it was a great big world, with lots of places to run to, and if she had to die tryin', she had one little promise she was gonna keep."[12] I had discovered

---

First Door: the main entrance, where 99 percent of people wait in line, hoping to get in. The Second Door: the VIP entrance, where the billionaires and celebrities slip through. But what no one tells you is that there is always, always… the Third Door. It's the entrance where you have to jump out of line, run down the alley, bang on the door a hundred times, crack open the window, sneak through the kitchen—there's always a way."

[12] Tom Petty & The Heartbreakers, "American Girl," track #10 on *Tom Petty & the Heartbreakers*, Shelter Records, 1976, vinyl

that I could explore the world by other means; relying more on divine grace, humanity's good will, volunteering, and trading my jewelry or massage services.

Granted, I no longer wanted to sleep on a bed of straw while being bitten by mites and fending off sexual advances from a complete stranger, but I had no desire to stay in five-star hotels either. I was happy somewhere in between; being able to rely on my income and ability to barter and staying somewhere within my means. I never stayed in *nice* places and certainly wouldn't have done so on my own, but if Matt was paying for this trip and that was how he wanted to roll, then I could do that too.

I knew he planned on traveling extremely light because he had asked me to bring his tiny zip off pack (which was part of a larger backpack) and his flip flops, so I followed suit. I don't think minimalism was even on our radar as "a thing" back then, but I quickly realized Matt was taking this to a competitive level. I packed my regular school sized Jansport backpack for our seventeen-day trip. I brought my Spanish dictionary to continue my studies, a Lonely Planet travel book, my hiking boots, and fleece jacket that I tied around my waist while in transit. Matt was both gloating about how small his bag was and poking fun at me referring to, "all the shit you brought," multiple times. He insisted my hiking boots, fleece, and Spanish dictionary were unnecessary. To "help me" minimize my load, he found a box and a local post office for me to ship these items back to Kodiak.

We stayed our first night in Playa del Carmen, Mexico in a nice place (by my standards) and then in a rustic but spendy bungalow on the beach in Tulum before taking the bus over the border into Belize.

We looked at property and had a blast in Caye Caulker, Ambergris Caye, Dangriga, and Placencia. We discovered we were more than compatible traveling together, and we absolutely saw eye to eye when it came to locations and property. We agreed Ambergris Caye was not our thing with all the golf carts and retirees. We enjoyed Dangriga as an authentic place to visit, but we both thought that it was "underdeveloped" as a tourist destination at that time. Placencia and Caye Caulker were much more our speed, but the recent damage from Hurricane Iris in 2001 was very noticeable. I found myself continually comparing Belize with the lush vegetation and wildlife of Costa Rica (specifically my favorite beach *ever* Punta Uva near Puerto Viejo) which was not affected by hurricanes.

We spent a lot of our time on the beach, enjoying the white sand and crystalline blue waters, but in order to use the shade umbrellas and chairs we would have to order food or drinks. This is how we discovered panty rippers (coconut rum with fresh pineapple juice). I was not much of a drinker, so after a few day-drinks, I was ready for a siesta. Matt could handle more, but when I caught him slurring and asking the waitress for, "Another rip your panties off," I knew it was time to take a break and return to our cabaña.

I turned twenty-eight in Placencia. Matt wanted to make my day really special, so he started it off by treating me to a massage and a body wrap. We had lunch at the upscale Turtle Inn Restaurant and then an afternoon swim with a few panty rippers before we headed to Kitty's Place for dinner. It was a perfect day, and we were both glowing, maybe too much so, from the alcohol. We had finished our meal, but it started to pour down rain, so we each ordered one more of our new favorite drink. After that, I was too ripped to stay there any longer. If I had another drink, I was in danger of physically not being able to walk back to our hotel. We decided to make a move for the gift shop downstairs to wait out the rainstorm and not continue taking up space in the restaurant. I could only look at souvenir magnets, plastic fish, and bird guides for so long before I had to pee, really bad. When I asked the cashier to use the bathroom, she informed me it was back upstairs in the restaurant. Too embarrassed and tipsy to return to the restaurant, I told Matt I would just go outside and then we could make our way back to our hotel down the beach. It was still raining, but not pouring. "Yah, you're going to do it, babe? You're really going to do it?" he asked, slurring as well. Living in Alaska and having spent much of my travel years in the great outdoors, this was not uncommon for me. Also, drunk in the rain at night, I really didn't see a problem with peeing right alongside a nice hotel and restaurant. But what happened next was completely unexpected. As I began to lift up my dress and squat down, Matt began to take all his clothes off not too far from where I was peeing.

"What are you doing?" I wanted to know, laughing and nearly losing my balance.

"I thought that's what *you* were doing, taking all your clothes off to run back to our hotel."

Just then, two new restaurant customers came walking up toward the stairs, so Matt began walking backwards, holding his clothes in front of his crotch, panicking and stumbling. I was laughing so hard as I pulled my panties up under my dress that the couple asked if everything was okay. I realized this was a rather strange scenario, and they may have misinterpreted my tears as distress, but I was *dying* of laughter. I reassured them that yes, everything was fine and thanked them as we began to run off together. Matt hustled to keep up since he was running backwards, still covering himself. The path we assumed would take us back to the beach opened up to a large pool area complete with a covered bar and stage for live music. Lucky for him, it was dark and empty. Now I could finally ask, "Why in the world did you think I was going to take all my clothes off?"

"I don't know, because you're an exhibitionist?"

This had been one of his running jokes. After I had shared with him that Jimmy (my ex-boyfriend) and I had stayed on a nude beach in Mexico, Matt and I had occasionally hiked to and sunbathed at what we started calling Nude Beach in Alaska. Throughout our trip in Belize, he had been teasing me about this by asking (in the most random places), "Are you going to take your clothes off *here*?" Usually, it was in a public place where no one, not one single person, was indicating nudity was okay. I had found this hilarious, but apparently, he thought there was some truth to this. I was doubled over crying from laughing as he struggled to get his clothes on, and then we both stumbled down the beach, laughing together as we held hands with the sound of the waves crashing and the rain on our skin. We were completely and utterly in love.

We had so much fun and things had gone so smoothly between us, that this trip was when *we knew*. Not everything had been vacation or easy for us thus far in our relationship. We had both been extremely challenged while he tried to navigate co-parenting (or the lack thereof) with his ex-wife, and we rode the emotional waves of their contrasting views as to what was in Gabe's best interest. But we both rode the storms of uncertainty together in the exact same way; united, trying our best to stay elevated, loving one another, and laughing as much as possible. It felt like nothing life (or the Universe) threw at us could bring us down. We talked about all of this on the bus ride back to Mexico, agreeing that it felt like we could overcome anything together. The more we spoke about the places we had been, what we liked and what we didn't, and the possibility of creating a future abroad, the more our dreams began to overlap, eventually merging with one another. By the time we returned to Playa Del Carmen, we were both elated and began popping in and out of the Mexican silver shops, trying on cheap matching rings that looked like wedding bands as an outward symbol of what we both knew; we wanted to spend our lives together. Glowing, we settled on two silver bands with wave designs etched into them. Matt told me these were just temporary because he wanted to officially propose once he bought me a "real" engagement ring. The next day, we held hands on the plane ride back home and were beaming with love as we admired our rings and basked in this newfound certainty. Creating a future together *was* possible. I thought to myself how interesting it was that it wasn't until I had declared that I was no longer looking for someone to spend my life with and had decided to focus on my own goals that I finally met the right person. This seemed to embody every 'focus on yourself first' dating cliche for single women.

Chapter 8

Don't Steal My Sunshine

Once we got back to Kodiak, Matt was exhibiting what I considered highly suspicious behavior. He was spending a lot of time on the phone in our bedroom, talking in a low voice. When he suddenly announced he was going on a spur of the moment trip to Florida, I assumed it was because he wanted to talk to my parents, specifically my father, before he asked me to marry him.

"That's very sweet, *and unnecessary*," I told him.

"What do you mean?" he asked, doing a horrible job of keeping a straight face.

"If you are going to Florida to ask my dad's permission to marry me, that is sweet, but unnecessary. I'm an adult woman who can and *should* make her own life decisions, *especially* major life decisions like marriage."

"I don't know what you are talking about," he said with a twinkle in his eye, pulling me in close to him to give me a hug.

"Michelle, I know you are an adult, and I respect that. We both know we want to spend our lives together. Let's just say that I *am* going to Florida to talk to your parents. Could it be that maybe I want to show respect for your family as well? That I want to start off on the right foot with them?"

"Haaaaah," I sighed, "That's the sweet part. But you don't really know them or that much about my rebellious past. My parents and I have never seen eye to eye when it comes to my life decisions. There is a good chance that they will say no."

He pulled away, looking concerned but said, "Babe, your parents really love you, and so do I. I haven't given them any reason to say no, and if they do, well, we will cross that bridge when we get there. I was really wanting to keep all of this a secret, and you're ruining any element of surprise." I rolled my eyes at him, spinning what he didn't fully understand (all the emotional pain I had caused my parents in my youth and young adulthood) around in my head. I knew that if they said no, it wasn't going to be about *him*; it was going to be about them warning Matt about *me* and my unconventionality that they viewed as selfish.

"Can we please change the subject?" he asked and I agreed. But once he left for Florida, it was the only subject I could think of.

I was a ball of emotions that fluctuated between being excited and curious to frustrated, afraid, and then annoyed. Annoyed with myself for being so head over heels about the idea of marriage. Annoyed with the ridiculous tradition of asking a grown woman's father for her hand in marriage as if I was some sort of possession. I would get excited about the prospect of spending our lives together and living abroad. Then, I would remind myself that I had never even imagined getting married. Although I had wanted to meet someone who was right for me, marriage was never the end goal. I had always thought that if something was forever, then it was forever, regardless of a ring or a piece of paper. For me, the divorce rate was proof that the institution of marriage was yet another illusionary sense of security. I didn't need those things to feel secure in a relationship, and I *never* wanted a diamond, that was for sure! So, I was surprised by how much this excitement had hijacked my mind and felt ashamed that I was so curious about the ring I assumed Matt was purchasing.

I was afraid of the conversation that might be going on about me and what my dad might actually be saying to Matt. My parents and I had some *unspoken* resolve about my teenage rebellion, but I imagined that was mainly because on the surface, I seemed to be getting with the program they believed in. There was a part of me that had admitted that I did need *some* money to survive, which honestly had felt like defeat. A little bit of my untamed spirit had died with that acknowledgement. I felt I was surrendering my soul to the system. I had caved in and then found a compromise, choosing a career in massage therapy. Having my own business had made me more responsible in their eyes but saying we had healed our relationship would be a stretch. We had mostly just buried the past, *but had we?* I felt I had found my own resolution in self-acceptance and by letting go of the need for their approval. I knew my parents were probably never going to approve of or understand my lifestyle one hundred percent. But disapproving of my life's choices was one thing. Voicing their disapproval about their daughter to her future fiancé was another. My dad was not the most diplomatic person in the world, so I had my panties in a wad, worrying about how much of his perspective regarding my "behavior" growing up he would *overshare* with Matt. Though I wasn't proud of hurting my parents, I wasn't intentionally trying to hide anything from Matt either. In the eleven months we had been together this just hadn't come up, but I had the feeling it was about to.

When Matt returned, I was trying to contain my anxiety and excitement about his upcoming proposal not knowing exactly what he had planned. A few days went by, and *nothing*. I reminded myself that the one-year anniversary of our first kiss was one week away and thought maybe he was waiting until then. But when he got a call from his boat captain saying they would be leaving to go out fishing late that night, it became obvious that we wouldn't be together on our anniversary. I couldn't hide my disappointment or the anguish any longer. Sitting on the edge of the bed, all of my emotions and built-up anticipation came tumbling out of my mouth as I began to cry about not being together for our anniversary and how I had thought he was going to officially ask me to marry him. He felt so bad. He explained that he had wanted to hike back out to Termination Point in Monashka to propose to me in the exact same place where we had shared our first kiss. He pointed out that I was being impatient and ruining any element of surprise *again*. Wiping my eyes, I let out a big sigh not knowing where any of this would leave us. I wondered if I would have to wait until he got back from fishing to hike out to Termination Point. He was right, I thought. I had spoiled his plan, and it seemed silly to even carry it out at this point. As I asked myself why being engaged had become so important to me, Matt interrupted my thoughts by tackling me on the bed. He pinned my hands down, and then gave me a huge hug and kissed my face, wiping my tears away. Looking me in the eyes, he asked, "Michelle, will you marry me?" He scrambled to get the ring from its hiding place. Walking back over to me, he opened a small turquoise box, taking out a sparkly Tiffany's diamond with a delicate platinum band. Getting down on one knee, he slid it onto my finger. I didn't know how to feel about the diamond and didn't even know what Tiffany's was, but I knew how I felt about him. The answer was, "YES, YES, YES!"

We chatted nonstop about where he had purchased the ring, our future, and my family, which it turned out, my fear was *absolutely* justified. After Matt had told my dad how he felt about me and that he wanted to marry me, my dad warned him that I was an extremely selfish person. Thankfully, Matt was shocked by his remark and defended me by saying that wasn't his experience at all. He told my dad just how good I had been to him and his son, coming into their lives selfLESSly. He said that my mom was quick to interject and point out that I was making efforts to change. But regardless of what my mom had said, I found it highly unnecessary to share this with my soon-to-be fiancé. The fact that my father felt moved to say this, told me that he hadn't healed or come to any full resolve about my reckless behavior in my youth. It hurt that he thought I was selfish, but the fact that he still hadn't let it go and there probably wasn't anything I could do to make it better hurt even more. Regardless if I had changed or not, I knew that having different values and allowing happiness to guide me was not selfish, but that was something they would probably never understand. Oscar Wilde famously wrote, "A red rose is not selfish because it wants to be a red rose. It would be horribly selfish if it wanted all the other flowers in the garden to be both red and roses."[13]

My emotions were heightened again, but Matt reassured me that it ended up being a beautiful conversation with my dad who told him the secret to a successful marriage is compromise. I sighed, knowing that I was past the point of trying to make my parents see things from a different perspective. That had never worked. As much as I had hoped that there had been some resolution, I realized there may never be. Sometimes the best we can do is just agree to disagree.

As time marched on, I began to sit with Matt as he researched property on the Internet, and now we began to develop more of our dream together. We knew we wanted to relocate to Central America first (probably Costa Rica) and *then* get married, most likely there. Matt would have primary custody of Gabe for the next six months, but when he was out fishing, Gabe would stay at his mom's house. We knew that Matt's fishing schedule was unpredictable, and when Gabe would go to live with his mom for six months, there may not be a whole lot of flexibility on her part to make up for lost weekends. If we were lucky, we might see Gabe once a month, if that. Matt decided that the best time to leave would be when Gabe was in his mom's care, and then hopefully, once we got established somewhere, they could redefine their custody agreement.

Matt *did* share my same sense of adventure and had a happy-go-lucky personality as well. Like me, he was comfortable living in the unknown. He was fine leaving for Central America without having a

---

[13] Oscar Wilde, *essay entitled The Soul of Man under Socialism*, 1891.

solid plan, and even more open to a full spectrum of possibilities. He was exploring the idea of living part of the year in Alaska and maybe still fishing part of the year if it was necessary to see his son and earn more money. I was dead set on completely relocating, at least for myself. After much discussion and researching airline tickets, we found ridiculously cheap roundtrip fares leaving for San José, Costa Rica in early December of 2004, but we would have to return before Christmas. We decided to purchase and just not use the return. We would continue to work and save until December, and then sell nearly everything we owned, essentially leaving on a one-way ticket.

Once our tickets were confirmed, we began to break the news to our parents and Matt's ex-wife. It went about as well as I expected. "Well, Michelle, if you want to live like a poor person with a dirt floor, that's fine, but that's not how I want to live my life," was my dad's initial response. With every new development in my life, I continued learning a little more. By this time, I imagined it wasn't his intention to be a joy suck, and I knew that he was just concerned for my wellbeing and my future.

I tried a new approach. Instead of getting defensive or trying to "make him see" things from my perspective, I attempted to have a deeper conversation about his actual feelings. "Dad, that sounds really negative. I understand if you are worried about me. Is that what this is about?" I asked, which was just met with silence. Oh well, I thought, proud of myself for trying. Then, I added, "As you know, not everyone is poor in Costa Rica. We don't plan on living like poor people. We plan on starting a business in tourism down there." That was met with more silence and then a final stifled, "Well, if that's what you want to do." It was exactly what I wanted to do, and just like Tom Petty's lyrics, "the sky was the limit." But I was sure my dad would hear the words "a rebel without a clue" in that same song.[14] Digging in deeper to try to have more meaningful conversations now seemed like the best approach to healing our relationship.

My plan to own a small piece of property and build a massage studio and apartment for myself was expanding to include work for Matt as well. We figured we would do something that involved massage therapy or wellness and spent a lot of our time discussing and brainstorming about what our new tropical life might consist of. We explored opening a juice bar together, a hostel with a juice bar, a spa, or a hotel and spa. With our budget, we imagined we would need to buy raw land and then build ourselves. Whatever we ended up doing, we thought it would include Matt helping in both the construction process and operating the business. We were planning on creating work for ourselves, so the fear of Matt *not* working had never come into our stratosphere.

We decided to make our going away party a two-keg indoor garage sale to give our friends the first opportunity to purchase our nicer belongings while sipping locally brewed beer. We put price tags on our Alaskan art, books, camping gear, skis, my basket collection, and Matt's surfboards. The big conversation piece was the driftwood couch we had made which Matt was (only half) jokingly running a silent auction on. We were really surprised when nearly everyone asked what Matt would do for work in Central America. It became clear that they viewed me as having a career I could take anywhere,

[14] Tom Petty & the Heartbreakers, "Into the Great Wide Open," track #3 on *Into the Great Wide Open*, MCA, 1991, vinyl, cassette, & CD

but having only known Matt as a commercial fisherman, they were outwardly concerned about what he would do for income abroad. Prior to fishing, Matt had a rich history of entrepreneurial endeavors. As a kid he had shined shoes at the local train station; he had been a DJ; owned a clothing business; and managed a clothing manufacturing warehouse in California on the border of Mexico. Matt and I shared the same can-do positive attitude and knew we could both wear multiple hats; as cooks, receptionists, hosts, whatever! As the night progressed, we described our loose plan to skeptical looking friends, many of whom wished us luck, making it clear that it sounded like a wild idea. It wasn't unusual for people to not want to leave the island or "the rock" as it was called. Some of the people we knew hadn't left for *years*, not even to go to mainland Alaska. The sentiment being that Kodiak was the best place on Earth and a beautiful nature reserve away from all the ridiculousness of the rest of the world. Anchorage was a bad idea, so Costa Rica without a plan was unimaginable. We did our best to smile through the unexpected criticism we were receiving from good friends. Our departure day came soon after.

We drove Gabe to preschool blasting reggae music and rocking out as was customary for the three of us, but once we were there, it was long hugs, some tears and a difficult goodbye. Matt told him that we would see him in a few months when he would be back to get him and bring him down for Easter vacation. Explaining that next time we saw him we would all be on a great adventure together in Costa Rica.

As we settled into our seats on the small Anchorage bound jet, we looked out at the dismal gray winter sky. I felt all the bitter sweetness of our departure, and like a metaphor for how I had been feeling and as was customary on Kodiak Island, the airplane headed full speed straight for the ocean. Just when it looked like we might not make it (with the negativity of my parents and Matt's ex-wife, the skepticism from our friends, and the difficult goodbye with Gabe), the plane lifted off, flying parallel to the beautiful snowcapped mountains with the ocean below. We were actually on our way! We were buzzing with a full spectrum of emotions; the heaviness of leaving Gabe, the relief of having made it off 'the rock,' and with excitement for what our future may hold. We held hands over the center arm rest and I snuggled into the familiar place on Matt's chest as we talked about applying the same feeling of "knowing" that we wanted to spend our lives together to this next leg of our journey. We didn't know how we were going to know when we found the right place or property, but we knew we would know.

Chapter 9

Discovering The Dream

We landed in San José and called a friend and business associate of my dad's whose contact he had shared with me as someone we could possibly call in an emergency, or ask to store some of our luggage until we got settled. I took this to be his unspoken support, and we were thankful to meet Carlos and his wife over dinner at their house. We kindly refused their offer to stay the night, excited to get on the bus and see Puerto Viejo together early the next morning.

Upon arrival, we rented a small house near Playa Negra from a woman I had gotten to know on my previous trip who I called my Italian Mother. Matt and I spent our days on bikes exploring the beaches, looking for plots of land with "for sale" signs, and talking with people about property. Like me, Matt was impressed with and drawn to the lush greenery of the jungle just inland from Playa Punta Uva. The roadside wild bananas, hanging vines, and flowers were stunning, but we soon learned the reason why the jungle was so pristine in this area. It was protected. This came as a complete surprise to me that the area I had held so dear in my mind all this time was located within the Gandoca Wildlife Refuge. Therefore, it was not titled land. Still, there were fence lines and for sale signs within the refuge, so we continued to inquire. We talked to a number of foreigners who either lived here, had built businesses, or were currently under construction. As we learned more, Matt and I both became mind-blown, but for completely different reasons.

Matt couldn't believe that people were taking such a huge financial risk by investing so much money on untitled land and on construction that lacked legal building permits that the government may decide to destroy or confiscate later. I had never really considered what titled land meant or the importance of it. I was just learning about ROP or the right of possession property that exists in Costa Rica. Speaking to people at length, they were all building with the faith that the government was never going to take their land. I was down with faith, especially if that was the general consensus. But what I found most disturbing was that people (outsiders no less) were completely ignoring the fact that this was a protected area for a reason. That reason was to *stop* development and protect wildlife. We brought this up to some really crunchy Ewok village style granola people who were creating an alternative community within the refuge, and they didn't see a problem with it. Their perspective was that they weren't a large-scale development and weren't cutting down any of the trees. Their intention was to live in harmony with nature, but unfortunately that was not everyone's objective as there were chainsaws running on other nearby "plots" of land.

Because this was where I had always envisioned living, Matt really wanted to help make that happen. So, he set up a meeting with a couple who were local real estate agents to try and gather any legal information or professional advice that people like the Ewoks may have been lacking. This professional couple took us one layer deeper, helping to explain the root of the faith that so many held here and they validated our hesitation. "When Gandoca was created it was unique in that it surrounded a number of small communities of [native] people who were allowed to remain in the park. For this reason, people who are building here believe they will be grandfathered in as well." The woman went on to explain that she personally didn't think that small businesses or single-family homes would be destroyed by the government. "Have you seen some of the resorts that have been built on the beach? *These* are the people who I think should be worried because so far, the focus of conservation has mostly been on the marine area of the park."

The bottom line was that no one knew how the government was going to handle the sale of land and construction in the refuge, not even the government itself. They said they had inquired with the government for a number of people who they were representing, and no one knew anything. ***Nada***. And this had been going on for nearly twenty years. Matt and I exchanged a mind-boggling look, and then he asked if their extravagant home (where we were) that overlooked Punta Uva was on titled property. It was. Then he asked if they would advise buying within the wildlife refuge.

"Well, plenty of people *are* doing it," was the husband's answer with slow hesitation.

"But would you do it, with your money?" Matt asked.

"I guess that would depend on how much I was investing, but no. No, I probably wouldn't."

So, there we had it. Matt asked what other real estate they had available, but I could hardly hear anything over the sound of my heart sinking. In my head, I began to say goodbye to my lush tropical toucan dream. The woman must have seen the look of disappointment on my face because she came over to me and while squeezing my hand, reassured me that there were plenty of other beautiful properties in this area. I thanked her, but I knew it wouldn't be the same.

We spent Christmas day picnicking on the beach at Punta Uva with my Italian Mother, her family, and the howler monkeys. Then we agreed to cross over the border into Panamá to have a look around Bocas del Toro before returning for New Year's. We buzzed around in boat taxis island hopping in this beautiful archipelago for a few days. Like Puerto Viejo, local residents are of African descent who speak a Jamaican style Patois. We loved the colorful wooden homes and picturesque beaches as well as the reggae and Rasta culture. But coming from Kodiak, we knew first hand that living on an island costs substantially more than the mainland, and it requires a lot more effort. It takes more time, money, and logistical energy to transport yourself and larger items such as furniture or building materials to remote islands. And if we were to live more remotely than the main island of Isla Colon, we would have to own a boat. I saw these badass foreign women motoring their small wooden boats all around, but I was thankful that the expense and maintenance of a boat wasn't appealing to Matt at all. As much as I love the water, I just couldn't imagine cranking up an outboard motor by myself and having to weather the rain or high seas just to get to the grocery store. We both also realized that we are social creatures, and we wanted to live in an actual community, not on a remote island all by ourselves.

On our way back to Puerto Viejo, Matt had a plan. We would get off the bus to buy bicycles in the town of BriBri, which is also the name of the indigenous people who live in this region and the language that they speak. Then, we would ride all the way back to Puerto Viejo so we would no longer have to rent bikes. He insisted that he had scoped out the terrain with this adventure in mind when we came through before, noting that we had climbed up the hill from the coast the whole way here. He figured it would be no problem cruising (literally because we would buy beach cruisers with no gears or hand breaks) all the way back down. Looking at the bikes, they had a basket where we could balance our backpacks, and he figured it was less than ten miles. I was all out of excuses, so I agreed. We headed down the steep, windy, asphalt road with me squealing the whole way. My feet back-peddled on the break the entire time and my arms shook outstretched, balancing my backpack in place for fourteen kilometers. We screeched past unbelievable jungle scenes; waterfalls; and a red, black, and yellow collared aracari toucan whizzing by right in front of us. It was both terrifying and amazing. I was so glad we did it!

Upon our return, it began to rain, and rain, and rain. There was a torrential downpour for *days*. It rained so much that the ground became too saturated to flush the toilet. The septic system and the earth simply could not receive any more water. Matt said he didn't leave Kodiak Island to live in a place where it rains even more. He did have a point (and that *is* actually true) but my defensive response was, "That's why it's called a *RAIN*forest Mateo (his name in Spanish and my new term of endearment for him)." But I was beginning to let go of the idea of living in this area all together.[15]

Even though we knew we may not settle here, we continued to enjoy checking out other people's ideas and gathering more information. At open mic night on Playa Cocles, we spoke to the hotel and restaurant manager who ended up giving us a tour of the place because it was for sale. The beach was too rough here for our liking, and the hotel was way over our budget, but we loved the design concept, especially the outdoor showers. He gave us some valuable advice and told us that six was the magic number. He said if we were to build or own a hotel, six was the minimum number of rentals we would need to actually make money and not just get by. Six would provide enough income to pay for our first world expenses such as plane tickets back home and for Matt's son. We kept this in mind as well as Café Rico, the quaint, open-air, healthy breakfast and lunch restaurant with its good coffee and book exchange as possible future business models.

We spoke to various people about buying our bikes before we left, but it looked like we may have to sell them to the bike rental guy we were trying to avoid. He said he would give us $80 each, even though they cost us $100 and were just a week old. That night, I put my bike inside the patio yet again, even though the railing was

---

[15] Fun fact: The average annual rainfall in the U.S. is thirty-eight inches of water per year. Kodiak receives EIGHTY-ONE inches, and Puerto Viejo nearly NINETY-FOUR!

only waist high, and I encouraged Matt to do the same. He maintained it was unnecessary and that unless we put them inside the house, they could just as easily get stolen from the patio as outside. I thought we *should* put the bikes inside the house then, but he disregarded my warnings of theft in this area. We locked up the house and went to bed. Early in the morning, we both woke up suddenly, but we didn't realize *why* until shortly after when we opened the kitchen's wooden service style window and saw that my bike was gone. It was as if I was purposely punished for my mistrust because it would have been way easier to steal Matt's bike from outside of the patio.

It was 5:30 in the morning, and the sun was just beginning to rise. "Come on," Matt said, "Maybe we can catch them. Let's go into town." We locked up the house and went running to the center of town, looking up from the bottom of the few dirt roads in the main neighborhood. We asked someone crouched down in the middle of the road if they had seen anyone go by with a brand new bike, not realizing they were busy smoking crack with their head hidden under a jean jacket. "No man," he said as he came up for air. "Sorry." He asked us a few questions and then basically told us we should give up. "Your bike is probably long gone."

We knew he was right, and for me this was a bummer of an unforeseen event, but since Matt was a father, all of this was way too much. Not only the theft, but in his opinion, the party and drug culture of Puerto Viejo was not an ideal environment to raise a child. "I'm sorry babe," he confessed. "I just cannot see this being a good place to raise my son or any future children we might have." Aside from loving the jungle in the Punta Uva area, I had never really thought about the town itself from the perspective of a parent, but he definitely had a point. Because of the crack cocaine incident, I had to concede this may not be "our place" after all.

Matt knew I preferred the rain to the weather on the pacific coast where it gets extremely hot and dry during their "summer" months, but he continued coaxing me. "If we go over to the Pacific and nothing compares to the jungle, beaches, and wildlife over here, we can always come back." I knew he was right, so we cut our losses and sold his bike to the rental guy before heading to the Pacific Coast.

Chapter 10

Written in the Stars

We half-heartedly looked at the island property Matt had seen on the Internet in the Golfito area, knowing boat life probably wasn't right for us. We poked around in the port town of Golfito as well, which like any port town is a bit dingy with the smell of motor oil lingering in the air but is nestled within a lush jungle backdrop inside the protected Golfito Bay. We went inside Golfito's free trade zone which is Costa Rica's largest duty-free shipping and shopping hub, but it seemed overrated to us. I had always loved visiting working class towns while traveling, so I was open to considering living amongst the hustle and bustle of everyday life. We looked at a few typical cinderblock houses for sale overlooking the port, but nothing really screamed *this is it.* Golfito is also the jump off point to the Osa Peninsula, the most remote and untouched area in all of Costa Rica, so we took the ferry to the small town of Puerto Jimenez which immediately felt more like our speed. The town itself was made up of a few thousand people, and it was also surrounded by beautiful jungle. We spent a few days, kayaking at sunset with dolphins all around us as well as watching monkeys and scarlet macaws right downtown.

Corcovado National Park was all the buzz here with both the locals and the tourists raving about all the wildlife in the park. After a few nights in Puerto Jimenez, we had already made friends with an American couple who lived there, and Matt had spotted a small piece of property downtown just one street from the main road. He told me there was a cement ruin towards the back that we could possibly utilize, converting it into a juice bar or my massage business downstairs and maybe a few rentals upstairs. He was so excited about it that he had already talked to the owner who lived right down the street and learned that he was asking $8,000. Since we had shifted our sights away from an area that I was familiar with, I was of the mindset that if we liked a particular place, we should at least spend a few weeks or possibly a few months there to get a better feel for it. *Then* we could begin looking at property. "If it is meant to be, it will be," I told him more than once.

I knew that Matt was hoping to find something (or at least our place) before he brought Gabe down in April so that we could start to establish some stability in his son's life. Standing in front of this small property, I could also see the potential through the overgrown grass and the ruin of an unfinished building. "What about having an oxygen bar?" He suggested. "Like the ones you see in airports? And then we could build a small hostel on top, with just a few shared rooms." I wasn't sure Puerto Jimenez called for an oxygen bar, especially with all its fresh jungle air, but I could see where he was going with it. And $8,000 for a lot right downtown was a heck of a deal. "Honestly, there is no way we could go wrong buying at this price. This town and the tourism here is only going to grow."

I knew he was right, but this seemed so sudden to me having only spent a few days here, that I pumped the brakes a bit, countering with, "We haven't even seen the park yet."

"I know, but from everything we have heard, we know it's amazing! There is more wildlife here than anywhere else in Costa Rica, even jaguars! We don't have to build here. It could just be an investment, or we could build a small business using the existing structure and still have enough money to build a house for ourselves somewhere else."

This was a beautiful place, and we were only scratching the surface, plus the people we had been meeting were great. "Ok," I agreed, and we eagerly walked to the local owner's house, ready to commit to a new life here.

The owner of the lot was a mechanic who emerged from under a car's hood, greeting us with a greasy handshake and some surprising news. Between now and the time Matt had spoken to him that morning, someone else had bought the property. This was disappointing, but clearly it was not meant to be. I suggested that we venture into the park so that we could experience it for ourselves and see more of the coast. "Who knows, maybe that's where we are supposed to be?"

Our new friends drove us out to Matapalo for the day to explore more of this pristine coastline, to look at some property along the way, and to introduce us to some wonderful people they had told us about who owned a spiritual retreat center. After a brief introduction and sharing the fact that we were looking for property, these people did not greet us with a warm welcome. To the contrary, they seemed quite leery of us, even after I flashed my own hippie-isms at them. I mentioned that I was a massage therapist and a yoga practitioner and Matt asked about the surf. We sat through an uncomfortable dinner that we were made to pay for, when it was clearly a friendly dinner party. After dinner, our friends took us to a more reasonable place where they had arranged for us to stay. This place had an ecological/esoteric feel to it as well, but our "room" could hardly be called that. There was only one full wall behind the bed that had a basic stick-figure painting of someone sitting in meditation with rainbow colored chakra circles along the front of their body. There were only half walls around the other three sides and a mosquito net over the bed. It was $70 per night with a shared bathroom! "Maybe because it's right on the beach?" Our new friends suggested, reassuring us this was probably the most reasonable place around. Grateful to them for having brought us there at all, we said our goodbyes and got a fairly restless night's sleep. The next morning, we walked the empty Playa Piro beach, which was absolutely stunning with nothing but coconut palms in sight. After that, we jumped in a *colectivo* and headed further down the road to the national park. From the back of this makeshift truck-taxi, we saw the other small luxurious hotels that dotted the hillside across the road from the beach which this area was also known for. Just before the entrance of the park sat the safari tents with Corcovado in the background and the ocean in the foreground. These tents were rumored to rent for $400 a night. Those were the options here: luxury hotels and extremely expensive glamping or camping inside the park, all at the end of a horribly maintained dirt road. We opted for just a day hike and then headed back to Puerto Jimenez, mind-blown by the land and hotel prices. We had been renting nice clean rooms with a private bathroom for $25 a night. $70 would normally put us in a three-star hotel, not glamping under a mosquito net. It seemed like everyone was banking on the undeveloped beauty and wildlife in this area. We discussed how a decent mid-range hotel would do well in this area, but from what we had seen, property was really expensive, possibly justifying the cost of lodging as well. This area was truly gorgeous, but it felt like the Hollywood elite of Costa Rica, in fact, supposedly Cameron Diaz was staying there at that time, which wasn't our thing. We thought to continue our search, reassuring ourselves that we could always come back here or to Puerto Jimenez if nothing else called to us.

I had been to Dominical and Uvita before and thought either one of these places could be the one, but the more we saw, the tighter our filter became. Being in Dominical again, I realized that the beach where the tourism was concentrated had hardly any local homes anymore. Aside from the school, there wasn't much of a national community here. The Ticos (as Costa Ricans are often called) I saw were working at foreign owned businesses, and even then, there seemed to be more foreigners working in Dominical than Ticos.[16] As we explored more, we learned that land prices were more reasonable on the other side of the highway where the

[16] Fun fact: The name Tico comes from Costa Ricans' widespread use of the suffix *ico* or *ica* to describe any and all things as small (*chiquitico*).

local population mostly lived. It saddened me to see this level of displacement, and it made us realize that we wanted to live in a place that had more of a local community.

Speaking to a real estate agent confirmed for us what we were already beginning to feel; we should have arrived twenty years ago. He was the first person who point blank asked us how much we had to spend, and although we felt a little uncomfortable telling him, it became extremely helpful. "Hmmmm you may not be able to afford Costa Rica," he said, suggesting we look into Panamá, which was cheaper *and* politically stable, or Nicaragua which was even more reasonable but possibly not so stable. Since I had a massage client and friend from Kodiak who was retiring with her husband in Boquete, Panamá, we decided to make our way to the border.

The second we entered Panamá, everything changed. The hot, old yellow school buses we had become accustomed to traveling in were now brand new air-conditioned Coaster buses. The pot-holed, dusty roads transformed to smooth asphalt highways. Panamá lacked the "Pura Vida" vibe of Costa Rica, but it was apparent that tourists were still a novelty. We found the people to be more curious and friendly towards us, always asking where we're from and where we were headed. We also noticed there was less petty crime. Our belongings felt safe on the bus, and we could leave our flip flops outside at night or our clothes on the clothesline without fear of them getting stolen, which unfortunately was not the case in Costa Rica.

Once in Boquete, my older friends were shocked that we had been traveling on buses for over a month now. After being in their rental car with them, we decided to follow suit and rent a car for at least one week. Using the Lonely Planet guidebook, we did a whirlwind tour of the country visiting the towns that interested us the most. We looked at property in Boquete and all along the coast, even crossing to the Caribbean side again to see Portobello. Venao was interesting to us with just four shacks on the beach and a thatched restaurant. Though the local population was spread out with no actual "town" and no evidence of foreigners, which forced us to ask ourselves if we wanted to be the *only* gringos. Nope, we did not. We took a couple of photos of *Se Vende* land signs with phone numbers and moved on. Nothing really called to us too loudly until we arrived at the small coastal village of Playa Joyita which literally means "little gem beach."

It was nearly a two-hour drive from a major grocery store, but it wasn't an island. The last stretch was freshly grated in preparation to pave the road to Joyita for the very first time. We stayed at a locally owned surf camp and walked the long stretch of black sand beach outside of town without seeing a single soul. Aside from one house on this beach, there was nothing. We daydreamed out loud about buying a piece of property on the bluff overlooking the water. The beach combing was amazing as well with lots of driftwood, shells, sea glass, seeds and (sadly) plastics.

There were a handful of foreigners living here from all around the world, but Playa Joyita was still an authentic Panamanian village. It was the social balance that we were looking for. This was primarily a surf destination and Matt was a surfer. There was one scuba shop that organized dive excursions to Coiba National Park, an UNESCO World Heritage Site, and I was scuba certified. With only five small hotels and five restaurants it was relaxed yet screamed potential. We ventured to Joyita Beach at night, and while holding one another, we looked up at the sky. The sheer number of stars were incredible! Matt pointed out the Milky Way which was right on top of us and said it felt like we were swimming in it. All signs were screaming YES! We would return the rental car and come back to stay indefinitely.

Chapter 11

Untitled

When we returned to Playa Joyita we rented a basic but large wooden house overlooking the beach. We began familiarizing ourselves with the village and brainstorming business ideas. We discussed what already existed and what was lacking, which was nearly everything. Joyita had a population of *maybe* five hundred people. It was not off the grid but because it was the last town at the tip of the peninsula, it was certainly the end of the grid. It was (and still is) the kind of place where the kids run around in their underwear riding sticks for horses and kicking around a deflated soccer ball, happy as can be. A place where horseback is still a common form of transportation and time stands still as people sit on their porches idly chatting with family members and neighbors about everything and nothing at all.

There were only two small "window stores" with *very* basic supplies. You had to crank your head around to see the inside, pointing and communicating in your best Spanish for the shopkeeper to pass you what you'd like to buy. There was no bank, no ATM, no post office, no doctor, no pharmacy, no phone lines, or Internet, but there were rumors of an Internet Café opening soon. There was just one pay phone on the corner "downtown" which was where the main road that led to Joyita Beach intersected with the road to the surf point and the surfing beach. With the main road about to be paved, there was a lot of speculation that Joyita was on the verge of becoming a booming tourist destination. This conjured a type of bittersweet excitement for both of us. On one hand, the quaintness of village life was what we had been looking for, so we wanted to experience that pre-boom for as long as possible. On the other hand, boom would be good for business, so we were excited by the economic opportunity this would inevitably bring some day.

The town and beaches of Joyita felt right for us, but it lacked the wildlife and the jungle that I had imagined living in. Joyita is a semi-arid tropical forest which means it is affected by a long dry season with no rain and then has unpredictable rainfall approximately nine months out of the year. There are rolling hills along the coast, but much of Joyita has been logged, so instead of old growth trees and jungle, it's more barren with cattle and farming. Living here would mean no sloths and monkeys in my backyard, so I was actively letting that go. But there was a familiarity here that already made it feel like home. The terrain reminded me a lot of where I grew up in Southern California in the summertime. The hillsides were covered with tall dry brown grass and the breeze was so strong, it was reminiscent of the Santa Ana winds we would experience in the fall. There were fires and smoke visible in the distance that we were told were controlled burns to "clean the land." It was February, and it was so hot that I had no desire to be outdoors in the middle of the day. While I relaxed in the house directly above the sea, Matt was a man on a mission. He was out pounding the streets, investigating for us both.

We were only there a few weeks when Matt found an empty wooded lot on the main street that was for sale. The only thing on the property was a small tin shack with a thatched roof. It had lots of trees and potential since it was "downtown" in front of the local school. He had spoken to the caretaker's wife twice and was told to come back during his lunch break. He needed my help to communicate with him in Spanish. The irony of my Spanish skills being in demand after having failed Spanish 1 in high school and repeating it another year was not lost on me in that moment. "So will you please come, Michelle?" Matt asked me again. "I don't want to risk losing another opportunity like the one in Puerto Jimenez. I think they are asking $15,000 and it has avocado, lime, and a bunch of fruit trees, but I need you to verify this. And I want you to come look at it with me." With the mention of fruit trees, I schlepped my sweaty body up off of the futon to walk the dirt road with him in the heat of the day.

We interrupted Señor Faustus's lunch with his wife and children in their simple open-air patio which also served as a dining room. He spoke slowly, shaking our hands, repeating his name, and explaining it meant "lucky." He gave Matt the small wooden children's stool he was sitting on and gently told one of his sons to give his stool to me. We insisted this wasn't necessary and explained we were interested in the land for sale. "Yes, my wife told me," he said dismissively as he sat back down on the concrete floor and continued eating his lunch. He motioned for us to take a seat as well. There was no visible hurry, so we began to settle in like the hot oppressive air itself.

Faustus chattered on in between bites, telling us how he didn't believe in luck. He believed in God, and he was a Christian. He then began to introduce us to each of his five children. Slowly we repeated the names we had never heard before as we tried unsuccessfully to pronounce them. Everyone laughed good heartedly. After their lunch, he walked us over to the land which was just two doors down from his home with his curious children all in tow. Faustus showed us around, pointing out all the fruit trees. "*Aguacate, limón, mucho mango.*" He provided us with more information about the property and its owner. The property was a sloped 1,000 square meters covered in a thick layer of crunchy dry leaves. It was titled, and yes, the owner was asking $15,000. He explained he had worked for the owner for a long time raking and caretaking this land, but she hadn't paid him in over five years. He had begun to pressure her to pay him for his services, but because she didn't have the means to pay him, she had decided it would be best to sell the land to pay her debt and receive the rest of the profit. Faustus could introduce us to the owner who was an older Señora who lived an hour away in the town of Soná. Matt and I sat and chatted together in English a bit while his kids ran around and looked at us inquisitively. Matt pointed out that having the school right across the street may be a good thing when discussing Gabe's education and a new custody arrangement with his ex-wife. Taking in the land, I noticed where we could build a few cabañas and possibly a garden café amongst the trees without having to cut anything down. The longer we stood there, the more we made small talk with Faustus asking about the school across the street and the ages of his children. We told him about Gabe and asked if he could go to school there. "*Si, si, si,* (yes, yes, yes)," he replied. "It's an elementary school."

As we acclimated to this leisurely pace, sometimes sitting in silence, I began to see a possible benefit of what Americans would consider an inefficient way of communicating. By not rushing, we were creating time and space for unforeseen questions to surface and for more information about the history of the property and the village to be presented. We had spoken with a few locals and internationals who were living there, but Faustus warned us about interacting with some of the people in the village saying, "Not everyone is good here. There are bad people too. You need to be careful when talking to people. Don't trust everyone." We agreed, telling him the same thing is true everywhere. But he insisted, "Playa Joyita is different." As he launched into teachings from the bible, it was difficult to know if we should heed his concern or if it was more directed at non-Christian people who spent their time drinking and sinning in general. He also pointed out the fact that if we were to buy the property, we could fix up the tin shack to make it nicer and have a rent-free place to live while we built something else. "I can help you with this," he added, suggesting that we dig a temporary outhouse. He also said he could help us get connected to the community water system so we would have water for bathing, drinking and cooking. "It will be easy. The community water cistern is above this land on the top of the hill. We can tap into the line right here." He pointed out where we could put a tarp up and cook outdoors temporarily as well. Faustus explained that it was customary for the caretaker to stay with the land, even after it is sold. "I'm familiar with the property and could help you with whatever you want to build. You guys want to build cabañas or something, no?"

The longer we stood there, the better and easier it all sounded. We discussed it in English, and Matt reminded me that he really wanted to get established to provide some stability for Gabe. "What if we offer him twelve thousand dollars?" he suggested. I assumed Faustus would have to ask the owner, and we would have to wait on a response. Thinking this could buy us more time as well as serve as a test to see if it was meant to be, I agreed and translated. "Yes," Faustus agreed, shaking his head excitedly right away. The owner would sell it for twelve thousand dollars, and by vigorously shaking our hands, we sealed the deal, unexpectedly agreeing to buy this piece of property.

Plans were made to go to Santiago on the bus together where we would meet with the owner, Señora Gladys and present her paperwork to Arian, an English-speaking lawyer who was the brother of a new friend we had recently met in Playa Joyita. Arian would help us to do due diligence on the property and write up a sales contract. Days later, when we arrived at Arian's office, we exchanged pleasantries and the Señora opened a manila envelope she had resting on her lap. We were shocked to see that her original purchase contract was a seventeen-year-old handwritten note on what looked like a cornucopia stationary/grocery list piece of paper, the type that come in a magnetic notepad that my grandmother would have stuck to her refrigerator. Though the pen had saturated the thinning paper, smearing and widening its details, it was still legible. As we expressed our concerns about this non-legal binding document to Arian in English, she continued presenting her paperwork, unfolding a surveyed plan of the property and showing us all the points and the names of each of the neighbors. Arian took his time methodologically explaining the situation to us as he clicked away on his computer further investigating this parcel of land.

"Okay, so this is *not* uncommon, having a note like this, especially from seventeen years ago. I have seen it many times before," he said reassuringly. "*But* this is *not* a titled piece of property, and it is not 1,000 meters as you had told me over the phone. It is 800 meters of what we call R-O-P, or rights of possession land, but it looks as if she *is* the owner here in the system." As we became increasingly more uncomfortable with all of this, the Señora smiled on, clueless as to what he was telling us in English.

After our experience in Puerto Viejo, we had both agreed that titled property was a must for us, so we all began to discuss in Spanish how and if we should still purchase the property. Arian further explained that the property could be titled, but as foreigners we could not title the property in our names. We had two options. We could either have it titled in the name of a Panamanian person or in the name of a Panamanian corporation which is commonly referred to as an "Anonymous Society" wherein we would be the actual shareholders, but that was the anonymous part. The name of the corporation as well as the board of directors is transparent, appearing in the government public registry, but the name of the shareholders remains anonymous and written within the body of the actual document that legally forms the corporation. We knew that an anonymous society was the common way of doing business here as a foreigner, and that eventually we would probably need to form a corporation.[17]

We spent over an hour in his office discussing our options and the costs involved with titling the property. It would cost us thousands of dollars and could take many months or possibly a year. Arian recommended we renegotiate the sale price to cover some of the expenses. After a somewhat circular conversation with the Señora not budging on her price, he suggested we continue the conversation outside of his office and told us he was happy to help with the sale contract and titling process if we were able to come to an agreement. We thanked him and asked what we owed him for his services. We were floored when he said, "Nothing." This is unheard of in the United States! He had shared tons of knowledge and legal advice with us and even worked as a translator, navigating this sticky situation with the Señora. Matt and I left his office beaming, saying *we love Panamá!*

We stood with Faustus and the Señora outside of the lawyer's office in the busy plaza and tried to explore other options in Spanish. "If you won't take less, what if we pay you a security deposit and *you* pay to have the land titled in your name? Then, we can finalize the sale when it's done."

"Ha!" She comically gasped. "Who knows how long that would take! I'm old. I could be dead by then." We laughed at her pessimism saying we hoped she would still be alive, and then the conversation finally became more personal. We asked her other

[17] This level of anonymity is what has given Panama its reputation as a tax haven and the basis of the "Panama Papers" scandal.

questions and she began to share more about herself, her age, and the property. She said she was sad about selling the land. She had always dreamed of building cabañas or something where her family could stay, but she never had the money. When she first bought the property, she would come to camp with her kids and grandkids on weekends and holidays, but she hadn't been to Playa Joyita in *years* now. "As the kids got older, everyone got so busy with their lives." We told her to come out and stay or see what we build if we buy it, but she shook her head saying it would be too difficult to see someone else realize her dream after all these years of owning the land. "I really need the money to pay Faustus and would like to invest it into my house I have here in Santiago."

The fact that *I*, as a twenty-eight-year-old American could come in and essentially build the dream that this seventy-year-old Panamanian woman was never able to realize saddened me. I didn't know this woman's story, but I assumed she had worked hard her whole life. Yet, coming from the U.S., it was clear how much of an advantage we had and how unfair this situation was for someone like the Señora Gladys. This was an aspect of buying property here that I had never considered. As Matt and I offered her $10,000 one last time, I realized this was not in *her* best interest as she had always wanted to build something on the land and only had one opportunity to turn her investment around. All of this hit me in real time as we used the fact that she had said the title process (or anything with the Panamanian government) could take *years*, not months. We mentioned that we probably wouldn't feel comfortable building anything there until it was titled in our names to justify lowering the price. "Okay," she finally agreed, shaking our hands, and we all filed back up the stairs to Arian's office once again.

The Señora's presence was not required for yet another lengthy (and also free) complicated discussion wherein Arian educated us on the two types of anonymous societies. One (which the majority of the board of directors was Panamanian) would allow us to do business here and title property. The other (which we would be on the board of directors of) would allow us to acquire residency. Not having a large enough budget for both, we opted to start with the latter, deciding residency should be a priority. We would move forward with purchasing an untitled piece of property and immediately transfer ownership to Arian, a man we had just met that day, but already trusted. He would title the property for us as a Panamanian in his name. We would move onto the property and live in the little tin shack, rent free, as Faustus had suggested, unintentionally making my father's worst nightmare come true: living like poor people with a dirt floor, though quite likely happily ever after.

Chapter 12

Rich Gringos

Just as I had always wanted to fit in while traveling, my vision for moving to Latin America included assimilating and being accepted within the local culture and community. I had always admired those stereotypical American expats who obviously lived in a place because they seemed to know everyone. They were usually overly tanned, barefoot, with baggy board shorts and an open buttoned-down shirt walking around with a beer in their hands and a smile on their face that emanated a *todo bien* attitude. That quality of life was what I was after, *not* the American dream. I wanted to live within and fully embody this relaxed culture where less was seemingly more and happiness wasn't purchased; it came from within. Finally having chosen a place to put my roots down, I imagined myself as the female version of this with sandals and a sundress, minus the beer, having the safety and security to be friendly and open with the members of our new community.

We were now living in what we affectionately called "the hut." Faustus taught us about the thatched roof as he helped us sweep the cobwebs and burn a small fire to smoke out the wasps that had moved in. We rolled out a large sheet of linoleum over the dirt floor and placed a cheap metal sofa bed on top of that where we slept uncomfortably with the metal bars in our backs. That first morning we awoke to lots of little eyes peering through the cracks and the holes of our rusty corrugated metal walls. Needing to use the bathroom, I pushed the skewed (also rusty metal) door open to find about twenty small children in their school uniforms with little backpacks in our new yard. "*Hola, me llamo Michelle*," I said standing there in my pajamas wanting to be friendly. They all giggled. "What are your names?" I asked, not knowing if I could possibly hear them all before I *had* to go into the jungle to use the shallow hole we had dug. This produced more laughing, shoving, and teasing one another as they told me, "His name is crazy pants," and other such silly things. "Okay, well you need to go back to school," I told them as they continued to push each other and crack themselves up, paying no attention to my instruction. I was hoping it wouldn't come to explaining that I needed to use the bathroom or them following me, but it did. I explained them away by waving my toilet paper roll around in the air and pointing to the school realizing we must be the most exciting new thing in the neighborhood.

Matt quickly became convinced that we needed to overhaul the hut by changing out the hot rusty tin walls to make it nicer. Faustus suggested we change the tin to the thin bamboo they call *caña blanca* which is cooler because it allows the air to flow between the canes. He explained that this is how everyone used to live until gradually people wanted more protection from the elements, insects, and animals. "We started building our houses out of wood, and then block, but those were hotter, so we started needing electricity for fans. Some people even have air conditioning, and from there it just became more and more," he laughed, shaking his head at this ridiculousness. "It's *better asi, verdad, más natural*," he said. Meaning, this is better to live more natural, don't you agree? I shook my head yes and thought that the more you have, the more you have to worry about. I realized that the little that we did have (Matt's computer, my camera, our wallets, money, and passports) would not necessarily be safe in a house made of sticks. Regardless, we decided this was the best temporary option until we built something else on the property, so the guys got to work replacing the walls one at a time.

We had no electricity, but had invested in a small fan that we could run off of our car battery that we had parked out front. We had bought a tiny panel van, like the ones that you see used for deliveries in third world countries that are not street safe in the U.S., and in the morning the battery would be dead. Our property was at the top of a small incline, so we could jump start the mini-van rolling it down the hill. One of our first nights in the hut, Matt woke me up in a panic saying he was getting wet. He thought something was peeing on us even beneath the mosquito net we were sleeping under. He shined a flashlight on the dusty old thatch ceiling, and there were bats hanging overhead. It was bat piss. I love my sleep, and I hadn't felt a thing, so I was in no hurry to get out of bed and deal with bats. Matt couldn't believe it. "Really!? You're just going to lay there and let bats piss on you?"

"Mmm hmm," I agreed, "I still don't feel anything."

"Well, I do, and maybe you can sleep through that, but I can't!"

"Huhhhhhh," I let out an exasperated sigh rising up off of the hard metal bars of the sofa bed. "What do you want to do?" I asked.

"I want to move the bed outside and sleep under the kitchen tarp," he said. "Just for tonight." We began moving our makeshift kitchen table out from under the tarp and put the bed in its place, essentially sleeping outdoors. The next morning, we woke up to Señor Juan who managed the town water system coming through the property to open the valve and send water to the entire village. We greeted him, having a laugh and asked what time it was, joking that he was our *alarma* or alarm clock. We realized that this may have been rare for two gringos to be sleeping outdoors like this, but most people were living simply here at that time. Many showered outside using the water scooping method; dipping a small container into a fifty-gallon drum in their yard, waving and greeting passersby as they lathered up their hair or armpits, usually in loosely fitted clothing or their underpants. We had repurposed our rusty metal tin to create a basic outdoor shower as well, but with real plumbing. We too were lathering and smiling. I was also washing our clothes by hand and hanging them out on the line to dry, which was all evidence to me that we were one and the same with the locals.

Having grown up camping, I was fine with all of this, probably more so than Matt. The only exception being when he went back to Alaska to get Gabe and there was something *big* scuffling around in the thatched roof in the middle of the night while I was all alone. Not knowing what it was, I made my way over to Faustus's house with a flashlight and woke him and his wife up asking for help with extermination. He followed me back to the hut laughing. Once there, he picked up a long PVC tube and began to beat the palm leaves, telling me it was probably an opossum. After not finding anything, he went home, but it was impossible for me to go back to sleep. After I had been still for a while, I heard it again, crunching around overhead and then finally I saw the opossum walk down the outside of the bamboo wall. It was right behind my head with its large silhouette and long rat tail in the glow of the streetlight in front of the school.

Panamanians have a great sense of humor and being in Central America for over six months, my Spanish was finally getting to a level where I could understand their humor and joke with people, too. I realized this was a huge part of my personality, and I was happy I could finally express this side of myself. We were learning that this humor was incorporated into the nicknames they had for one another in Joyita, and nearly everyone had a nickname. Most were still the names they were given as babies or small children, and many times it had to do with their appearance. There was *Gordo* (fat), *Rosita* (Little Rose who was no longer small at all and in all actuality should have been called Extra Large Rose), and Ron Pico (which apparently was slang for little dick, so he was Ron with a Small One). The list went on and included plenty of others that were equally entertaining. One day, as I was washing our clothes in the large cement sink Matt and Fausti (Faustus's nickname that we had begun using) had installed, a girl about my age came walking up to the hut saying a quick hello. She then launched into a desperate plea, "My baby is hungry and I have no money. I just need a few dollars to buy milk for my baby."

This was something I had never anticipated. I was concerned for her hungry baby, but I was probably more concerned that she saw me as a financial resource and wondered how many other people viewed us in this way. "Why do you think I have any money?" I asked her, truly offended.

"I don't know, because you're a foreigner?" She shrugged looking puzzled, like *duh*.

"Yeah, well, look at the house I am living in," I told her, knowing the hut was hardly evidence that we had money. "Plus, I don't even know your name. It isn't as if we are friends."

"Ahhhh," she said. "My name is Mireia," putting out her hand. "And you're going to build a nicer house for yourselves, no?" she asked.

"Hola Mireia," I struggled to remember and pronounce her name. "Mi nombre es Michelle," I said while still shaking her hand.

"Do you like flowers?" she asked, looking at the bare ground all around the hut.

"Yes," was my slow reply, already seeing where she was going with this.

"I will bring you some flowers," she stated. "You will see. We will be friends." I shook my head no, not to friendship, but to her empty promises.

"You really don't have a few dollars?" She looked at me skeptically because let's face it, of course I had a few dollars. "My baby is hungry," she reminded me. This was not something I wanted to navigate. Of course I wanted to help people in need, especially starving children, but there was something about this woman that I didn't like. Perhaps it was her directness or the fact that she was targeting me that I didn't like. Either way, my body and mind were still telling me no, so I stuck with that.

"Sorry, I can't at this time. Maybe in the future, *si conocemos mejor* (if we get to know each other better)," I said.

"Okay," she let out a deflated sigh. "I understand. I will bring you some flowers. You will see. We will be friends."

"Okay," I said, happy to have closure. "*Te espero*," which means I will wait for you, but *espero* also means hope. In that moment, it hit me how ironic this is. In the English language, if you are waiting for something, you are probably hoping for it, but these two words are not synonymous like they are in Spanish. I was beginning to see that there was a lot of simultaneous waiting and hoping for things to materialize for us in Panamá: the title for our property, our residency, even a plan. We had found ourselves unexpectedly idle with all of this *esperando* when it would have been nice to move forward.

The possible fate of Mireia's hungry baby was weighing on me, as was the fact that we might somehow be perceived as rich gringos. Later when I saw Fausti I told him about my encounter with Mireia. He shook his head no, chuckled and asked, "You didn't give her any money, did you?" After reassuring him that I had not, he told me, "Good. Don't! *Her* nickname is *La Rumba* which means The Party. She was not going to buy milk for her baby with that money. She was going to buy beer for herself in the

Cantina!" And sure enough, later that same day I saw her on the back of one of the new scooters that were being rented in town, beer in hand, having a great time, waving to me as she whizzed by. And no, she never brought me any flowers, and we never became friends. This was confirmation that I had done the right thing because if I had given The Party milk money for her baby, how often would she stop by asking for more? I began to wonder how much we realistically could open the charity floodgate to others and if that would be part of being accepted here. How would I know who was truly in need or who to believe? I remembered Fausti's warning that we couldn't trust everyone and decided to adopt a tough-love policy, at least until I began to form real relationships.

Matt and I had agreed we wouldn't invest in construction until our property was titled in our names. We had also agreed we should spend more time getting to know the village and the land before we started building. We talked about waiting until the rain came to consider water flow, drainage on the hillside, and the direction of the wind. But once he and Fausti finished fixing up the hut and had even mixed and poured a cement floor together, he became restless. Matt began to discuss our building strategy all day, every day. There were no free standing, private cabañas in the village with air conditioning and real hot water, only what everyone referred to as 'suicide showers' with the electrical wires inside the shower head itself. So, he suggested we build what would probably be the nicest rentals in Playa Joyita. "We could live in the first one and build at least two more. Then, maybe we could build a garden café with a gift shop." I was on board with all of this, *eventually,* but maintained we should wait until the property was titled.

Matt insisted we should break ground sooner than later to avoid spending through our savings. But it wasn't until Matt started to talk about the need for parking that I began to feel terrible about actually building here. I heard the Joni Mitchell song, "Don't it always seem to go, that you don't know what you've got 'til it's gone, they paved paradise and put up a parking lot," in my head, and I visualized the impact that we could have on this community.[18] As some of the first foreigners to build on Mainstreet, we had the potential to be the beginning of the end; the start of a town that will eventually be completely changed and overrun by tourism. I wondered why I had never thought of this before, but the truth was I had never imagined settling down in such an undeveloped area. My original dream of owning a simple massage studio and having a bike for transportation had been in a touristy area, and it *didn't* include parking. This new awareness that *I'd* be the one paving paradise was heart breaking.

"If it's not us, it will be someone else," was Matt's perspective as he began to shift from pressuring me about building the cabañas to, "let's *just* build a retaining wall where the restaurant would go." This was our first argument *ever*. I listened to him explain that "It will create so much more property and won't cost that much *or* be a main structure" about twenty times. Finally, I just gave in so I wouldn't have to hear it anymore. He clearly needed another project to focus his energy on way more than I did. We hired Fausti full time, and a father/son team to build the retaining wall. Matt was buzzing all

---

[18] Joni Mitchell, "Big Yellow Taxi," tack #10 on *Ladies of the Canyon*, Reprise, 1970, vinyl

around the property and going back and forth to Soná which was the closest place to purchase building materials. He was basically doing circles around me in the hammock tranquila, reading my book.

My project had been to mosaic tile the floor in the hut as practice so that later I could add mosaic tile work to the hotel and restaurant. I had invited Fausti's children over and together we tiled a Sponge Bob, a pineapple under the sea, fish, and a surfer riding a wave. But this was not something I could do (or needed to do) eight hours a day, and soon a second argument broke out. Matt wanted me to sketch out some plans for the cabañas and the restaurant, but I remained adamant that we should wait, refusing from the hammock which did not land well. "So, you're just going to spend your time in the hammock and not help me then? You're not going to do this to *help us*?"

"Nope, not at the moment," I coldly replied barely looking up from my book. I could see a pattern beginning to form. He couldn't sit still waiting and hoping, and I was holding my ground that we should continue to wait and hope that the property would in fact be titled in our names before we invested all our savings into the construction. He was highly motivated. I was moderately me. I turned another page with a smug look on my face and he got the picture, so he walked away with nothing resolved.

Chapter 13

The Wild West

The first incident we experienced that clued us in to the fact that we were now living in a lawless society was centered around gringo Donald. Donald was an American expat in his fifties who was rumored to have photos of naked underaged girls from the village (yes, children) on his computer. He liked to show them to anyone who was interested. Everyone comically called him McDonald, which I'm guessing was due to his name *and* the simple hotdog and hamburger restaurant that he owned called The Forsaken Cafe. We had met McDonald within our first few days in Joyita, and we could tell right away that his personality exuded the same cynicism as the name of his cafe. He looked like Raoul Duke's character in the film "Fear and Loathing in Las Vegas" with his Panamá hat, mirrored sunglasses, and cigarette hanging sideways out of his mouth. His sentences were all warnings that started with things like, "These people," and ended with, "fucking crazy" or some such variation. As he leaned in over his laptop where presumably his pedophile photos were, he told us, "Give them an inch, and they'll take a mile." I immediately became uncomfortable with his blatant racism especially when I considered the fact that we were all "guests" in this country, therefore we shouldn't be speaking poorly about a culture or community of people who are essentially hosting us. This kind of cynicism from foreigners living in a foreign land is quite common, but my view was that we needed to either be respectful of the local culture and people or leave if we don't like it, but don't complain about it.

Within a matter of minutes, I had had enough. I thanked him for his incredibly negative opinions and walked away with Matt right behind me and McDonald shouting, "I hope I didn't offend you." I made a mental note to *never* become jaded by the local culture like McDonald, knowing that was not possible, not to that degree. Later when Fausti told us something similar in Spanish saying, "*Dar la mano y toman el brazo* (give your hand and they'll take your arm)," I wondered if there was any cultural truth behind his slanted remark.

The next American expat we met here was also named Matthew. Later he was nicknamed Hippie Matthew for his long graying hair, gunslinger style mustache, and John Lennon glasses. He told us he was in the process of buying The Forsaken Cafe, which sounded like good news to me. He said he had given McDonald $25,000 in cash in Arian's office which had promptly sent McDonald on a multi-day drinking binge in Santiago. Apparently while inebriated, he was pulling huge wads of money out of his backpack which people noticed, including the taxi driver who dropped him off at his hotel. Later that night, two men forced their way into his hotel room, tied McDonald to a chair and stole some $10,000 worth of his money. Prior to this happening, he had managed to invest in a small fleet of mopeds that he was planning on renting (one of which The Party was on). Attempting to make his way back to Joyita on a moped, which was an incredibly dangerous and windy two-lane road, he wrecked and returned with a few broken ribs and a broken collar bone. For me, McDonald's negativity was the dark cloud that seemed to follow him, and Hippie Matthew affirmed this opinion in his own way saying, "That guy is an accident looking for a place to happen." McDonald began renting his mopeds for $3 an hour. No one in the village respected this man, and they quickly began to run his bikes into the ground which we witnessed firsthand from the vantage point on our property. The last streetlight in the village was just past the school and the hut, so at night that became the designated turn around spot for people on McDonald's scooters. Almost everyone would stall the bikes as they slowed down, and then struggled to restart them, kick kick kicking the gas pedal, all of which was extremely audible through our breezy new bamboo walls.

One night, McDonald was extremely drunk, and while driving his sedan up and down the grated dirt road, he began peeling out, laying on the horn, and screaming out the window. Apparently, he was in a tizzy because his local girlfriend had another guy on the side (Fausti's brother in-law) and was yelling for him to come out of his house while swinging a machete around. It was one in the morning, and he had now successfully woken the entire village up for this. It was impossible for us to sleep with the epicenter of this dramatic event only two doors down. "MARCUS, MARCUS!" he screamed, with the metallic sound of the machete hitting the ground in between rounds. He got in his car and began skidding around again, doing donuts at the bottom of the main road in front of the town beach. Then, he would return for another machete screaming match with himself. Eventually, Fausti came running over, sneaking through the neighbor's yard behind our property and asked if Matt or I could drive him to the police station in the next village before something bad actually happened. Matt agreed, saying he would go, and the two of them left in the *busito* (what we called our little van). I laid there awake, a little worried for my own safety, while they were gone for what seemed like an eternity. Finally, I saw a small procession of cars returning, and Matt turned into our driveway and came back inside the hut. "Hey," I whispered, "What happened?"

"The police didn't want to come," he said.

"WHAT!? WHY?" I couldn't believe it.

"They were getting dressed to go but then once Fausti told them that the gringo had a machete. They got scared and said they *couldn't* go because there were only two of them."

"But that's their *job*! They're policemen! Aren't they trained for that!? Don't cops always go with their *partner* in twos?"

"I dunno babe," he said as he started getting undressed to come back to bed. "They said a gringo with a machete is dangerous. It wasn't until Raúl showed up and basically told them they *had* to come and that McDonald was injured and wasn't going to do anything, that they got in their car and followed us back."

Matt was exhausted and fell right back to sleep, but I was still on red alert, peering through the bamboo as the village became eerily quiet.

In a town of 500 people, this was all the buzz the next day. McDonald had also been renting out his sedan for extra income and Hippie Matthew went to where he was living early that morning to rent his car, completely unaware of what had happened. Matthew pounded on his door repeatedly until McDonald finally answered, holding himself up in the doorframe for balance, looking haggard and totally hungover. The first words out of his mouth were, "They tried to kill me last night."

"*Who* tried to kill you?" Matthew asked.

"*Everyone.* The entire village."

Hippie Matthew explained all of this to us later, laughing in disbelief adding that, "His car rides like shit now." He told us that while McDonald was driving around like a drunken idiot, people were throwing rocks and beer bottles at his car trying to stop him and as an outward expression of *their* drunken disapproval. I had always imagined a lawless society would be a utopian society, but now I was beginning to have my doubts. Admittedly, I found all of this slightly entertaining, but I couldn't help to wonder just exactly what we had signed up for here.

Shortly after the McDonald incident, the locals had another nickname for our busito; *la ambulancia.* This was because it was boxy and white looking like an ambulance *and* because it was now doubling as one as well. We hadn't realized it, but our car was one of about six total vehicles in the village at that time, and one of the only vehicles that was located in the center of town, right between the two Cantinas. One Sunday (which we were learning is a big drinking day), one of our construction workers showed up at our doorstep, bleeding and holding his bicep. He had been at the Cantina when someone threw a broken bottle across the bar, and it cut him in the arm. He asked if we could drive him to the hospital. I jumped up and wrapped his arm in a towel, and Matt grabbed the keys, speeding off to the hospital an hour away. But while they were gone, I began to get angry. The cut was bad and blood made Matt extremely nervous. I knew he would be driving like a bat out of hell to get him to the hospital as quickly as possible, so I became worried about Matt's safety on the dangerously windy road. I was angry that someone who had been drinking in the Cantina was now putting Matt's life in danger. When Matt got home safely, I was relieved, but I told him I thought people needed to drink at their own risk. I was not going to drive anyone to the hospital from a bar fight. "I'll drive women in labor (which we both had done) or kids with broken arms, but I'm not going to put myself at risk and take hours out of my day because someone *chose* to put themselves in that situation."

My days were actually busy now because the more time we spent here, the more we had come to trust that someday Arian would indeed have our land title. After giving in to Matt's insistence, the construction of our first cabaña was fully underway, and I had magically become an architect overnight, drawing some basic sketches for the first two rentals that we wanted to build. I understood aesthetics, space, and design and was hand drawing everything to scale to make sure doors would open, windows made sense, toilets would fit, etc. Matt showed me where to draw the more linear aspects that I didn't know I had to think about and didn't want to think about. Boring things like the plumbing and electrical tubes.

He thought about ceiling fans, grease extractors, and porch lights which never would have occurred to me on my own. We were able to get building permits using what we coined my *kinder-drawings*, meaning kindergarten. Matt began managing our construction crew, learning more about cement and block and the Spanish that went along with it. My job became all the legal red tape that was involved in relocating and opening multiple kinds of businesses. There was a lot involved in dealing with Panamanian bureaucracy which due to inefficiency and archaic record keeping, felt as if the hands of time were moving backwards.

It was as if the busito was an ambulance *and* a time machine, and the two-hour drive (one way) to these government offices was a portal to a land of Brother typewriters, dot-matrix printers, floppy discs, multiple hand stamped carbon copies, and file cabinets whose drawers dated back to the 1970's! A huge amount of patience was required for all of this, as well as all the cultural sensitivity I could muster to not become cynical like McDonald. Yogic breathing helped along with Fausti's good humor and his mantra "*poco a poco*," meaning little by little (you will get everything done), which he would tell me regularly. There were many days that I would return home exhausted from the four-hour drive, speaking Spanish non-stop, and feeling like barely anything had been accomplished. The worst was when the government workers I needed to speak with were not in their office, and I was told to come back tomorrow. "*Come back tomorrow when I live two hours away!? **Impossible!!!***" I'd end up losing my patience and raising my voice. "Why don't *you* come to Joyita tomorrow?" I'd asked sarcastically. This would undoubtedly provoke a defensive response because it was, "*muy lejos* (very far)".

"*Exactamente* (exactly)," I'd say, leaving completely exasperated.

"*Poco a poco*," Fausti would repeat yet again or, "*todo con calma*," which literally translates to "everything calmly" but means "take it easy" insinuating that everything will happen in due time.

Aside from being unruly, the people from Joyita were extremely resourceful. Matt and I marveled at their simple solutions to remedy problems that would have required a trip to Soná or Santiago. One day I had a splinter in my hand and no tweezers or needle to get it out, so Fausti went over to a citrus tree on the property and cut one of the sharp thorns from a branch. He washed the natural needle and then proceeded to pick my splinter out. When the wheelbarrow had a flat tire, the construction workers set to work removing the tube and locating the hole. They asked me for string, which I also couldn't produce, so Fausti pulled a loose string from the bottom of his tattered shirt, unraveling it even further as he yelled, "*Aqui, ve* (here look)." cracking us all up with his childlike innocence. Bunching up the hole, they took the string and wrapped it super tight, isolating it from the rest of the tube. There was lots of hollering, asking, and running around, but eventually Fausti retrieved his bicycle air pump that he had loaned out to someone in the village and the tire was refilled. They told Matt their work was a temporary fix, and he should add a patch and tire tube to his materials list. "*No garantizado*?" Matt jokingly asked. "*No garantizado*," they responded, and we all laughed. Matt and I admired their ingenuity. Similar techniques were applied as we expanded our water system and realized we had the PVC water tubes and glue but lacked the unions we needed. *No problema*. The guys showed us how with a lighter or a small fire, you could heat up one end of the tube, softening and expanding it, so that another could fit inside. "*Listo y frito*" (fried and ready, or all done), as they commonly said here. I loved learning these expressions and saw the value in their resourcefulness living so far away from "civilization." These were the satisfying moments when I felt like we were connecting with and learning from people in the community.

What I had loved about Latin culture when I was traveling was that it was so raw, open, and in the street for everyone to see. But now I was realizing that included death and catastrophe as well. Within that first year of living in Joyita, Matt and I had both seen dead people on the side of the road. Matt and Hippie Matthew had seen an electric line worker hanging dead from his harness; upside down, swollen, charred, and still smoking, having been electrocuted only minutes before. Shortly after, a school bus full of children passed and knowing these kids would all see the same thing, Matt started freaking out, now in tears. He said they needed to try to stop the bus. Hippie Matthew couldn't believe it. "Haven't you ever seen a dead body before? Get a hold of yourself man! I've fucking pulled needles out of friends' arms who ODed on heroin! Seriously. We have shit to do. We're not turning around. Do you need me to drive?"

I saw two dead people on the side of the road with their windshield wrapped around their necks and everyone from grandmothers to children in the small town where this car accident had happened were running to see, which made me realize just how different peoples' view of death is here. There was no one covering the bodies until the ambulance arrived, and only God knows (which was also a popular saying here) how long that could take. Although the newspapers and tabloids do not make it to Joyita, it is not uncommon to see dead people on the front page or to be shown on the Panamanian news. Fully recognizable graphic images that the family or friends of the deceased could potentially see are broadcasted.

When a friend of ours in Joyita stabbed another local resident at a fun-loving Italian girl's birthday party, we understood that these incidents weren't just confined to the Cantina. After a great party at Hippie Matthew's new oceanfront cabañas, someone broke into one of his rooms, resulting in an altercation that led to his Canadian guest needing stitches for the huge gash across his forehead. I was never for *defunding* the police. I was N.W.A.'s "Fuck tha police," all the way, so it was crazy when I hand delivered a letter in my best Spanish to the governor's office in Santiago explaining the growing tourism in this area and the need for a local police station.[19]

[19] N.W.A, "Fuck Tha Police," track #2 on Straight Outta Compton," Priority; Ruthless, 1988, vinyl, CD, & cassette

Chapter 14

From Shit to Sunshine

We were building much like the way we had chosen to live in Joyita: "Make it up as we go along, feet on the ground, head in the sky, it's ok I know nothing's wrong," adding structural support and new creative features as ideas came or the need arose.[20] As an afterthought, we began to excavate behind the new cabañas just outside of the tropical open-air showers to install a small leach field where the shower water could drain into. We built the showers right on the edge of the neighboring property line which we had thought nothing of, but someone from the village did and they took it upon themselves let the owner of the property (who we had not met yet) know.

We knew and loved our neighbors who lived to the left of us, in fact we always shouted, "*Vecino!*" or "neighbor" to greet one another. *Guapo* (which meant handsome) was from the village and was helping to raise his wife's two young children who were from a neighboring

[20] Lyrics from The Talking Heads song "*This Must be The Place (Naive Melody),*" track #9 on Speaking in Tongues, Sire, 1982, vinyl & cassette

island. When we first moved into the hut, he asked if he could climb up a tall mango tree on the edge of our property to install a television antenna which he had mounted in a long bamboo post to try to get better reception. We shared laughs about his overweight climb, and his wife yelling to him from inside their house as he repositioned his device in the tree and the picture got substantially better or worse. He was a fisherman, but when Matt would ask him if he caught anything for the day, he would laugh and say, "No, only women." Matt asked his wife how she felt about this, and she shrugged, not seeming to care. So, their running joke became that while Guapo was out fishing for women, Matt would go visit his wife. Now that we had moved into the larger cabaña we had built, our kitchen window overlooked their backyard and a 50-gallon drum/shower. We would see his stepchildren bathing or usually crying next to the tub in their underwear because they didn't want to bathe with the cold water.

The lot to the other side of us was empty, but the neighborhood kids would play baseball there and come ask us for water before, after, and during their games. We were told the neighbor behind us was an affluent Panamanian who owned the entire hillside (some 15 hectares or 40 acres of land), and he was unhappy about us "building" on his property. I felt horrible about this and became nervously fixated on the problem, over discussing it with Matt and Fausti. Fausti reassured us that Rey (his nickname meaning King because people jokingly called him the king of the hill) was very nice, telling us not to worry that he knew him well and had worked for him for many years. He pointed out that we hadn't actually built anything on his land and was confident that once he came and saw for himself that there was nothing (because the leach fields were already installed and covered), it would all blow over. But I found his name alone to be unsettling, and that is not what happened.

Rey kept us in an uncomfortable state of uncertainty for nearly a week. When he finally did show up on our property, he was briefly cordial shaking our hands and then turned to Fausti and asked him to walk him to the back of the property. Fausti began to explain away the situation by being truthful about what had been done, but showing him that it was no longer a problem, as there was nothing left to see. Rey dismissed this and turned to us instead, speaking in English. "You *do* know that there is a legal easement in Panamá?" He asked us. We shook our heads no. "You cannot legally build a permanent structure within 1.5 meters of the property line, and if you want to build a fence or a wall, you need to speak to your neighbor and get their permission before doing so." Matt interjected that because the showers were open-air and therefore *less* of a permanent structure, we hadn't thought it was that big of a deal, but he rolled right over him. "I have spoken to my lawyer *and* the mayor," he continued, "and so you know, the mayor might be coming here to inspect the property, along with some people from the municipality and the police." Great. I began to panic, imagining both of us being hauled off to Panamanian prison.

"We're really sorry," I spoke for the first time, clearly alarmed. "We had no idea, and we certainly don't want to have problems with any of our neighbors." Feeling like I was about to cry, Rey presented us with a solution which may not have to involve the authorities.

"Look, I know you're good people."

He did? I thought. How?

"I'm sure we can work something out," he conceded.

Oh good, I thought as I breathed a sigh of relief.

"What's probably going to end up happening is you will need to hire an *agrimensor* to measure the land you encroached on here and pay me for this parcel so that we can keep the 1.5 meter easement between us."

Hmmmmm, my antennas went up.

"I'll give you a fair price of $10 a meter. If you agree to this, then I won't have to involve the authorities, who by the way, will say the exact same thing. You will need to compensate me for this." He added that it should only be 100 meters or so, costing us $1,000, and he felt confident that the three of us could take care of it on our own together. Matt told him that because we are new to Panamá, we wanted to verify the law with our attorney which led to a more friendly conversation about Arian, his sister, and their wonderful family. We got his contact, and then thanking him and apologizing yet again, we told him we would be in touch soon. "Don't take too long. The mayor told me he would be here in a few days."

The next day, Matt and I headed to Costa Rica to do a border run since our tourist visa was about to expire again, and we still did not have our residency. We called Arian on my mini cell phone that only worked outside of Joyita once we were in route. He confirmed both; that the easement law was true and that having to pay for the property *was* the most likely outcome. He reassured us that as long as we cooperated, we would not be going to Panamanian prison. He pointed out the bright side that we would have something to show for it (more property) in the end. Once we knew we probably weren't in grave legal danger, we had more room to become irritated. We spent the next hour of the car ride reviewing all the dirty details of the situation. As we saw it, there was another option. Rey could just forgive us since he owned 40 acres of land and was never going to use that small portion of property that he had no actual access to. Together we explored whether he really had spoken to the mayor or if he had been bluffing and whether we were willing to take our chances.

Discussing things with Matt sometimes felt like a mental chess game. He was always looking for solutions and trying to think ahead by anticipating the other person's next move and the outcome of each possible choice. This type of attempt to predict the future was new to me. It seemed to partly echo all the group sports he had played in his youth, that I had not, and was a much more strategic view towards life than I was used to. In fact, Matt had told me more than once since we had been in Joyita to not show people my cards or my hand, meaning to not give too much personal information away or tell people our business ideas. I entertained his ideas, talking through possible future scenarios, but I knew that ultimately, we couldn't predict the future, and I was of the mindset that if we are clear and open about what we want, there was a higher possibility of obtaining it.

He talked about stalling methods or avoiding paying Rey all together. "We could meet with the mayor and just see what he has to say," was another one of his suggestions.

I began to explore in my mind what it was that we truly wanted. "*Or,*" I said thinking out loud, "Like Arian said, we will be getting more land. That's what we had wanted all along because we were hoping to build six cabañas but don't currently have the space.

What if we ask Rey if he would sell us *more* land than the 100 meters behind the showers? Going up the hillside, possibly to include the clearing with the ocean view?" I became tickled with this idea, realizing just how revolutionary it was. I looked for the classic Grateful Dead song "Scarlet Begonias" to play on the iPod and sang along to the lyrics, "Once in a while you get shown the light, in the strangest of places if you look at right," seeing this as a way to completely turn the situation upside down.[21]

There was a path from our backyard that the community used to climb up the hillside and access the town water tank. I would go up there regularly to do yoga on top of the cement tank, to enjoy the view of Joyita Island, and the sunset. Below the tank, there was another little knoll that had space to build on with a beautiful ocean/island sunset view as well, and there was plenty of land between there and our existing property to build more rental units or some sort of spa or wellness facility. We were both discussing potential future scenarios with the excitement of building a house with an ocean view for ourselves someday being the cherry on top.

This was exactly the sort of self-serving information Matt would advise me to withhold. "*But*," he started looking ahead again, "We should just ask him if he would be willing to sell us a larger parcel going straight back and not mention the ocean view. We can get an idea of how much land it is by measuring on our own before we talk to him, and then when the surveyors come, we

[21] Grateful Dead, "Scarlet Begonias," track #5 on *From the Mars Hotel*, Grateful Dead Records, 1974, vinyl

need to make sure they include that piece with the deal." Eager to get back home to measure and get this deal rolling, I agreed.

When we talked to Rey, he was pleased with this turn of events that was clearly in his financial favor. He told us we would need to pay to have the contract drawn up and for the surveyor to measure and draw up the plan, which we agreed to. The contract was already signed when the surveyors came, and we discovered that we had underestimated the size, or perhaps they had measured too wide. Our prized piece was not in the 2,000 meters we had estimated it would include. Matt had to then climb up the hill together with the surveyor to point out the section that we wanted to be sure to include it in the plan, which he in turn, must have told Rey about because he wanted to inspect it. After he did, he told us that the property was no longer $10 per meter, even though he had already signed the contract.

He and Matt went around and around because as Matt pointed out, he had already agreed to it, and there was no way we could pay his new asking price outright. I watched as a verbal tennis match ensued. Rey said he could finance us with the original price as a down payment, and Matt began to negotiate interest free terms.

"Three years at $700 a month."

"One year, $2,000 plus whatever that is a month."

"Impossible. Two at $1,000."

"Eighteen months, and that's it, my last offer. That's the best I can do."

Matt and I looked at one another knowing that we had our hearts set on this. There was no other ocean view property available to adjoin to our existing property. We also knew interest was extremely high in Panamá if we were to take a bank loan (like 7%). We nodded to one another in agreement, not even discussing it or knowing what the chances were that we could fight it since we already had a signed contract. We shook his hand. A new contract would need to be drawn up, and steep monthly payments would follow. Never in all our hypothesizing did we foresee that hand being dealt, and I did wonder if it would have been better if we had just been open and honest about what we had wanted. But overall, this was a minor setback. We had managed to turn our little roadside lot into an ocean view property with enough land to complete our dream. Life was good. In fact, that's the name we had landed on for our business; *La Buena Vida* (The Good Life).

With this unforeseen event and expense, we could no longer move forward building the garden café we had envisioned. Matt began to question if he should return to Alaska to go fishing, but for me, that wasn't an option. That was our old life and speculating on that didn't feel like looking into the future. It felt like going backwards into the past.

La Buena Vida had become a huge art project for us and a labor of love. We were inspired by Mexican design and used lots of brick, wrought iron and wood accents along with brightly colored tiles especially cobalt blue, lime green, and mandarin orange throughout our construction. I was putting all of my mosaic experience to use on a larger scale, and Matt was utilizing the skills he had learned while working on fishing boats like plumbing, welding, and electrical installation. Anything we weren't sure about we would ask Hippie Matthew who was a retired U.S. contractor. He had so much knowledge that Matt started calling him "The Encyclopedia," which Matthew would reliably respond to by saying, "Yeah, I'm only missing a few pages."

Our property was on a gentle slope, and I had built mosaic planter beds around a lot of the trees which I decorated with broken vintage-looking tile and topped with adobe bricks. I enjoyed filling these and learning about the tropical plants and flowers which everyone walked by to get to our cabañas. We had an adobe brick path leading to the rooms, a miniature lamp post, and handmade Panamanian roof tiles that made it look and feel like a tiny artisan village. Each of our rentals was its own mini villa, painted a different color with a distinct theme. In the ocean villa that we lived in, I had mosaiced a turtle sink in the bathroom and two whimsical looking humpback whales surrounded by stars around the mirror. In the butterfly villa, I created a butterfly shaped mosaic mirror as well as added butterflies and insects to the countertop and the thresholds. The bird villa had a mosaic grandmother tree with a variety of birds in her branches and green parrots flying overhead in the alcove ceiling. When my family came to visit for the first time, my mom brought lots of fabric down that matched the themes in our rentals along with a sewing machine. She got to work sewing beautiful ocean, butterfly, and bird curtains, pillowcases, and accessories. She sat with Fausti's wife and daughters patiently teaching them how to use the machine while she simultaneously practiced her Spanish. My dad went out diving in the national park and though he wasn't happy about the distance and the quality of the basic local boats, he was thoroughly impressed with the quantity of fish that he saw. Overall, they enjoyed the local culture, got a kick out of Joyita, and were outwardly impressed by what we were accomplishing. My dad was full of questions for Matt regarding the technicalities of building and my mom was oohing and aahing over all the details we had included. Laughing, my dad called Joyita "Peyton Place" explaining that was the first American soap opera series full of small-town drama. He could see that was part of everyday life here. This was a real turning point in our relationship, and it felt good to hear my mom say she was proud of my sister and I for the women we had become.

Just as Matt and I began to wonder how we would be able to fund the rest of our project, Hans the Austrian Scuba shop owner introduced us to his cousin and her friend who had bought property in Joyita. They were looking to build a small hotel as well. These women were also impressed by our place and full of compliments. They asked if we would consider building something for them. This was something that hadn't occurred to us, but we were obviously enjoying this work and were really good at it. After speaking with them at length, we were absolutely interested. Matt would manage their construction, and I would help them with the decorating details and add mosaic tile work to their rooms as well. We agreed on a percentage and a plan to move forward, receiving yet another unexpected gift that reinforced my longtime belief that if your heart is in the right place, risk will always be rewarded.

Chapter 15

LTD Living the Dream

We were doing it; we were living the dream! We had been in Joyita over two years now and were carving a nice little alternative lifestyle out for ourselves. We had finished the construction of three cabañas (we were still living in one) and had begun renting out the other two. Matt built two other rentals for Hans's cousins that had generated enough income to start the construction of our garden café, which was now quickly morphing into an idea for a healthy breakfast and lunch restaurant. He and Fausti were building most of the structure together by themselves. Matt was welding all of the columns and the roof trusses which included incredible wrought iron rising suns with rays shooting out for support. Everyone could tell when he was welding because the lights would flicker from our place down to the main corner of town. This was a giant open-air structure that was nestled in under all of the trees, some of which we incorporated by cutting holes through the roof so as to not cut anything down. Everything was under the shade, so the plan was to use clear roofing and hang lots of plants to make it feel like it was still completely outdoors. The only cement structures were the kitchen and the reception and Fausti was blocking up the kitchen all by himself. Matt and Fausti were adding bricks around the arched doorway and windows of the reception which would double as the gift shop.

We had great friends! Though we knew everyone in the international community, and we all mostly got along, it seemed like there was a tendency for everyone to gravitate towards those people who they shared a common language with. My best girlfriends were European. I had an English friend who worked as a dive instructor, and she and I would do yoga together regularly in the evenings. My Spanish friend was a free-spirited tattoo artist and micro-entrepreneur. I spent a lot of time with Lena, a German woman who had arrived one year after us with her husband to build a hotel and restaurant up the coast in a neighboring village though she was living in Joyita. Lena and I were on the same learning curve, so we regularly shared information with one another as to how to go about breaking through all the red tape in a country where I was now discovering laws and procedures changed *dramatically* with every new presidency. This was affecting everything from immigration laws and the coastal land titling process, to how and where we paid certain taxes. It would be the U.S. equivalent of the IRS changing its name, function, and procedure every four years. Because Lena was getting ready to move on-site to her business, and Matt and I were preparing to open the restaurant, she and I were trying to take advantage of as much of the free time we still had as possible. We would get together for morning bike rides to the beach where we would stretch and swim, chatting and joking that our lives as we knew them were about to be over.

I didn't know the slightest thing about working in a restaurant, much less *owning* one, but I knew it was going to be *a lot* of work. For this reason, and countless warnings against it from friends and family, Matt and I *had* been hesitant to open a restaurant. But with no one in town catering to tourists during the day, we viewed offering healthy breakfast and lunch options practically a social obligation. The main restaurant in the downtown area was a thatched-roof open-air establishment on the corner that sat behind the local pay phone, which was the nexus of the community. But they usually served fried fish, beef, and chicken (if you were lucky) *for breakfast!* Eggs were a great challenge here. Pancakes didn't exist, and ironically, with all the fresh tropical fruit available, fruit salads were not a thing either. So, we planned to offer breakfast burritos, fruit salads, and homemade granola for people like us who did not want fried fish or chicken for breakfast.

I was a really good cook, and it was something I enjoyed, so we figured we would put that skill set to use as well. We *mostly* shared the same vision for the restaurant construction; however, we could not come to an agreement on the flooring for the restaurant. I had my heart set on Spanish floor tiles, and Matt kept talking about huge slate rock slabs. In my mind, those would be a pain in the ass (or impossible) to clean and would not match the colorful tile motif I was busily creating. We continued to add beautiful details in and around the dirt floor that would remain until one of us budged or we found a compromise.

We both knew we needed to open the restaurant sooner than later, but we were also in the midst of planning our wedding at a beach resort near Panama City. After having been engaged for a few years, and with no wedding plans in sight, our parents had started asking us if we were ever going to get married. Matt and I had wanted to finish La Buena Vida and then tie the knot in Joyita so that friends and family could come see our place and experience where we live. When we shared this with both sets of parents, they all insisted that since Joyita was a six-hour drive from the airport, it was too far, and no one would come. I found this really discouraging and neither of us believed it was true, but I began to shut down. I could see that planning a wedding was going to be a modern-day rite of passage, apparently one where the bride and groom's vision didn't really matter. I reverted back to "if it's forever, then it's forever," telling Matt that I didn't need to have a ceremony at all. His first wedding had been really small with just their parents and his brother in attendance, so he wanted more friends and family to be present this time around. He asked me to please remain open to this.

While we were visiting in the U.S. both of our families suggested a few venues outside of Chicago near where Matt grew up and where I had a lot of family within driving distance. We looked at these places but they were ridiculously expensive, and we agreed that they in no way represented who we were, our lifestyle, or where we lived. I was just about done when my mom suggested finding an all-inclusive resort near Panama City that would be easier for people to come for a weekend. That way I wouldn't have to do anything. They would take care of it all for us. The more I thought about just being able to hang out by the pool with friends and family, maybe even for four or five days, the better that felt, especially when I compared it to meeting and greeting three hundred some people in the Midwest.

Since I had never actually pictured my wedding, I was pretty unattached when the planning began and I chose my dress, the flowers, catering, and the cake. My mom came to Panama City for a long weekend, excited to be part of all of this. She was astonished at how smoothly everything went, especially how quickly I had found a dress in the first store we went into. She marveled at my Spanish and my navigational skills in the chaotic city. As the day got closer, and some of our friends and family started arriving to Joyita, I felt myself glowing in gratitude for all the people who would be present on our special day and for Matt and Gabe who had added so much to my life. I began to step into the realization that this really *was* a momentous occasion worth sharing and celebrating. We were both beaming as we read our own vows to one another. Gabe presented us with our rings, and we gave him a family medallion that had three rings on it that he could wear around his neck. Arian officiated the ceremony with over sixty friends (both new and old) and family members in attendance on the beach.

Though married life didn't look that different from the outside, as we settled back into our alternative lifestyle, I was surprised to discover that our marriage *had* actually conjured a deeper level of commitment to Matt and Gabe that I now felt within me. This was an extra layer of protection that I felt, knowing that we had both pledged out loud to always stand by one another even throughout difficult times.

Gabe was going to school in Alaska and spending ten weeks every summer with us. Matt and I had talked about having more children, but I still wanted to travel, and there never seemed to be an opportune time to be pregnant. A few of my close girlfriends were beginning to start families here, and we had talked about doing it together, but something inside me was telling me not to, that I wouldn't have a healthy baby. When I shared this with Matt, he said that he had the same exact feeling. My fear came from the messaging I received growing up about drugs, and the fact that I had taken so many mind-altering substances when I was younger, but his was just a gut feeling. Now I know there is no evidence that past use of drugs can cause birth defects. Years later, when I heard Michael Pollen say that LSD is less harmful to your health than drinking Dr. Pepper, I had felt duped! Not because this may have led us to not having children, that was fine. Trusting our intuition, the population, and the state of the world were all additional reasons to not have kids. I was more upset because I realized that as an advocate of weed and psychedelics, they *had* gotten to me too. Some of the 'war on drugs' rhetoric had, if not washed my brain, managed to give it a slight rinsing. *Fuckers!*

Being a stepmom to Gabe gave me the opportunity to experience motherhood which I was (and am) extremely grateful for. Some of my girlfriends told me, "It's not the same," which I assumed was because they wanted us to start a family at the same time as them to raise our children together, and *of course* I knew this was true, but I found myself feeling hurt and taking this remark personally. I would joke and say, "No, it's better because he came into my life potty trained," but their statement felt as if they were disregarding my role as a mother in Gabe's life and to me, it lacked respect for our decision to not have children. I certainly didn't want to make these women feel bad for deciding to have children and wished the respect was mutual. I was also of the opinion that being a stepmom was difficult in ways that these women would probably never understand, and I hoped they would never have to. Gabe and I had a beautiful relationship. In many ways we were closer than he was with his dad. Matt was continuing to do odd jobs outside of La Buena Vida to help finance our project. He was off building, welding, and installing things, as well as facilitating land sales for other people, so Gabe and I spent more time together during the summers than he actually did with his dad. As a mother figure he would come to me first for everything; at night if he was sick, when he was hungry, to ask for permission to drink a soda or to go on a bike ride. When we would play games all together Matt was so competitive and talked so much trash that inevitably Gabe would lean in and whisper to me, "Michelle, it's you and me against dad, okay. No matter what, we can't let him win." I'd agree because we *were* a team and together we'd read books, create art, go to the beach, and share lots of hugs, kisses and love. I loved him like he was my own, but he never would be. And this is just the tip of the iceberg of the unconditional stepmother/stepson love dynamic. Trying to co-parent with Matt's ex-wife who we were unable to agree with on *anything*, was a type of heartache and required a level of letting go of control around Gabe's wellbeing that my married friends who were starting new families of their own, *happily married*, couldn't possibly imagine.

I began to shift my mindset towards our hotel and restaurant being my babies, realizing that our debate about the flooring in the restaurant had drug on for so long, it was probably just a stalling method to delay the inevitable; becoming restaurant *owners*. Friends continued to circulate through the restaurant "area" and watch our progress, sometimes from the hammocks. I'd offer them a cold beer, and knowing all too well about our floor dilemma, they'd chuckle as they asked if we had made a decision yet, and when we were ever going to open. After months of this, we finally arrived at a compromise choosing a polished concrete floor as a temporary solution, knowing that at a later date, we could always lay rock, Spanish tile, or anything else we decided over that. I began to prepare myself mentally and emotionally for having a restaurant as I set to work trying to hire staff, starting with a woman who had been coming to my local art workshops.

After we had moved out of the hut, we had converted it into an art studio where I tried my best to host weekly community art workshops. I wanted it to be an intercultural exchange wherein we shared a variety of art techniques with one another to inspire methods for generating income with little investment. Matt and I thought that once we opened the gift shop, this could be an outlet to sell community artwork. I was sharing my materials and building local relationships as we did beadwork and crocheted recycled shopping bags. We made soda tab jewelry, tire tube purses and wallets as well as created decorations using driftwood, seeds, and shells. I had really hoped to learn from and empower others by facilitating *them* sharing traditional handicrafts from this area, but sadly, aside from the mention of *tembleques* (the beautiful Panamanian beaded hair combs which were a national thing), no one had any idea of something we could make that was distinctly from Joyita. I poked and prodded, asking about the bowls I had seen made from gourds, the large baskets the men sometimes carried on their backs called *javas*, clothing, *anything!* They made self-deprecating jokes about the only thing the people knew how to make here was *guaro*, or *chicha fuerte*, which was a corn alcohol people fermented in large vats usually in their backyards. So, I plugged along as the sole instructor with a solid group of ten or twelve men, women, and children who would come together to create things and converse with one another. These workshops really filled my soul and gave me the feeling I *was* building peer to peer relationships, *friendships* in fact, possibly not just being seen as "the rich gringa."

The first young woman I approached to work with me in the restaurant was someone I was close with from this group. Her name was Emelia. She was twenty years old with two kids, had a great sense of humor, and a little 'tude. I considered her a friend and was excited to be able to offer her work, and by the prospect of working together.

"Yes," she told me she could help. "As long as you don't expect me to open the fridge *and* cook on the hot stove."

"Actually, I do… why?" I wanted to know.

"Because going from hot to cold can cause you to have a *derrame*."

"I don't know what that is," I told her, so she explained. From her description, I concluded that she must be saying a stroke; that going from hot to cold too fast can cause you to have a stroke.

"Hmmmm," I thought aloud, not wanting to discredit her. "This would be a problem because I don't think I can hire two cooks right now. A refrigerator cook and a stove cook would probably be out of our budget. Whoever I hire will probably have to do both."

"All right," she said, "I understand," standing up to leave as if it clearly was not going to work out between us.

"So, you don't want the job?" I asked, taken aback by this strange turn of events and feeling really disappointed.

"It's not that. I'm very grateful for the opportunity, but I wouldn't want work to affect our relationship, and I definitely don't want to have a stroke."

I laughed out loud. "Emilia, I have never heard of having a stroke from a temperature change like that and especially so young! You are too young and healthy to have a stroke." Emilia was reluctant but did join me in the kitchen for a short while. This was the first of many "old wives' tales" I would learn about in Joyita and the beginning of the wave of local employees that would come and go, teaching me patience and diplomacy on a whole 'nother level.

I had fun filling the gift shop with local art from our group, souvenirs, and beachy things, and although it was a huge commitment, the restaurant was running fairly smoothly. With a thirty second commute, I could roll out of bed at 5:45 to begin prep with our two staff members (a cook and a waitress) at 6 a.m., and then open to the public at 6:30. I wanted people to be able to grab a coffee and something quick to go before they got on the 7 a.m. bus. Our place was the only place to get a smoothie or a salad in all of Joyita, and once we added a to-go lunch menu for dive trips, things were in full swing with a line at the bar in the early morning for people wanting breakfast and a lunch pack. We had quality food, first-world service, good music, and great ambiance. Friends were always coming through, as well as people from all over the world who would chill out on the giant couch we made, page through our book exchange or surf magazines, eat, chat, and laugh as they made meaningful connections. I was overseeing the restaurant, hotel staff and operations. We had managed to pay Rey off for the second property, and Matt was continuing to expand La Buena Vida by overseeing the construction of our fourth cabaña. He was the handyman and would fill in by waiting tables or in the reception whenever it was necessary.

Things ***were*** *todo bien* (all good) though the work was seasonal, which I was not used to. This meant during the dry season we were slammed, especially during the holidays, working twelve to fourteen hour *demanding* days. And then in the "winter" or *invierno* as everyone called the rainy season, especially during September and October, there were no tourists. This was a good time for us to travel, but "moderate me" would have preferred to work moderately throughout the entire year. And I probably would have preferred having a budget clientele because one thing we didn't realize about having more comfortable rooms, is that our guests were not of the shoestring traveler variety. In general, they had higher expectations for not only the rooms, but for the town and the infrastructure (or the lack thereof). It was 2008 and phones, cell phone signal, or wifi was yet to come to Joyita. We had an Internet Cafe in the village and a website, so we would check our email fairly regularly for reservations. But the majority of our hotel guests were "foot traffic" arriving without a reservation and a travel book in their hand. Still, we had amazing guests come through, and sometimes we would sit and talk to them for hours. Matt was especially good with people, finding something in common with everyone and was always friendly and happy. I required more alone time than him and preferred to be behind the scenes at times; in the gift shop, working more with the local population, or hiding out in the restaurant kitchen. Overall, we were well on our way to accomplishing everything we had set out to do (even more so), and we were still relatively unaware of the inner workings of the village.

Chapter 16

The Dive

I've heard living in Joyita summarized as follows: The first three months are the honeymoon stage; it's paradise and everything is great. The next three months you begin to realize there are a lot of problems; both resentment from the local population and interpersonal conflicts. The next three months *you* become the problem and find yourself at the center of some sort of conflict.

For me, the honeymoon stage lasted a little longer; maybe nine months or a year. But I didn't realize the extent of the resentment from the local population towards the foreigners until I started attending local town meetings. Meetings were held right across the street at the school, and the first one I attended was regarding the local water committee and the reelection of their board of directors. Water was a hot topic in the village because the gravity system had problems reaching certain areas of town. The valves were only open for about an hour a day so it was a matter of collecting as much water as you could within that time. This is the reason you see plastic blue holding tanks at each home (if they can afford it) or 50-gallon drums for collection in many countries because they do not receive water 24 hours a day, so they need to have their own private water reserve. As everyone began collecting, the quantity and pressure would lessen, and some people would go days or sometimes weeks without receiving water. Nearly everyone was affected by this in some way, and they were not happy about it, hence the election to see if they could improve the overall system under new management. Living right below the village reservoir, we had less issues than most, but whoever was elected would be utilizing the trail that ran directly through our property to access the holding tank and the valves. Fausti was going to run for president, so as someone I knew and trusted, he had my vote, and I decided to go to the meeting.

The meeting started nearly two hours after it was scheduled to begin. When I began to see more movement at the school, I crossed the street and found my way into a child sized wooden desk with a plastic chair attached towards the back of the classroom as an observer. More people continued to show up, filling in the seats and then standing against the walls. Eventually people were lined up outside as well, leaning with their arms poking through the open-air block windows as they peered in. Maybe they were too shy to come in, or maybe they just wanted to witness the spectacle that was about to unfold. Because soon enough, voices were raised and shit began to fly.

From what I could gather, there wasn't enough money to pay the electric bill for the well pump and the electricity was going to get cut unless they could raise more money or people with outstanding bills paid their debt. The room erupted as the people who owed money screamed about their personal situations, refusing to pay for a resource that they didn't receive. Someone suggested they raise the price of water for local homes from $1 to $3 a month and nearly everyone began shouting all at once demanding to know why they should pay more for such an unreliable system. When things calmed down, they began to publicly shame the debtors by writing their names and the amount they owed on the large chalkboard at the front of the room, but this led nowhere. Someone yelled, "Raise the cost of water for the businesses!" And a proposal went up on the chalkboard to change the fee for businesses from $5 per month to $20. This caused more upheaval but now from the foreign population who also didn't reliably receive water. Business owners insisted that a family of ten used more water than a small restaurant or a three-bedroom B & B that didn't have guests or customers year-round. They shouted that many of the local homes allowed their tanks to overflow as well, wasting water, whereas most foreigners had automatic floats in their tanks that prevented this from happening. "Make it mandatory that everyone has an automatic stop on their tank" and "charge per person in every household" were the demands from the foreign population.

Everyone continued to shift blame and responsibility for some time until one person finally walked to the front of the room declaring, "NO MORE FOREIGNERS ON THE LOCAL WATER SYSTEM," and the expat population went berserk. I could not believe this! I thought of where I grew up in Southern California near Los Angeles. I thought about New York City and how the United States was founded by immigrants. I pictured a large apartment building in a U.S. city that would not allow their immigrant tenants access to *water* because they weren't from there. *The most basic human need*! It was unimaginable! That would never happen! Verbal warfare continued as the foreigners pointed out that it was because of us that the system worked at all. We were the ones who actually paid our bills, and many times, donated money to help fix water tubes or pay the electric bill for the pump.

I was appalled by *everyone's* behavior and didn't know how they would manage to move forward, but they did. They found a compromise by establishing criteria for a small business ($10) and large businesses ($20), and it was determined that the price per local home would remain the same $1 per month. From there, they moved on to electing the new board of directors, and we were told foreigners were not allowed to vote. However, they did appoint a foreigner to be in charge of cutting people off (*literally* handing him a hand saw and some PVC glue) of the water system who owed more than three months. Fausti was voted in as the president. They elected the secretary and treasurer, and the meeting was adjourned, but I was fucking traumatized and the words "no more foreigners on the water system" rolled around and around in my head for days, making me realize I was now the *them* of us and them.

I should have stopped there, but the next meeting I went to was a training that the National Tourism Authority was offering so I somehow thought it would be different, and it was, kind of. It was better organized, but the presenters were met with the same rough and tough anti-foreigner attitudes. The Tourism Authority started by presenting basic skills for working in this industry. Things like being pleasant, saying hello, and smiling. Then they began talking about cultural tourism and the fact that people come here to experience Panamanian culture; whether it's local food, a conversation, art, or a tour. "Tourists are wanting to interact with *you, with Panamanians*, not an American hotel owner," which I absolutely agreed with. From there, one attendee began to express just how hard it is to get the capital to open a restaurant or build a hotel. "We don't have the same kind of resources to compete with foreign businesses." This sparked so much emotion and chatter that the Tourism Authority lost control of the room. I could absolutely sympathize with this and knew it was true that I had come from the land of opportunity. *However*, it occurred to me that maybe they were thinking too big, and I began to voice my opinion.

"But you don't have to start with anything that big," I said over the chaos that now simmered down to listen. "There are mangoes falling from the trees and rotting on the ground here. You could sell *chicha de mango* (mango juice) and just have to buy some cups and sugar, or *not*. You can make it natural. Charge fifty cents or a dollar a glass. Make a cardboard sign. You can start small." I envisioned a typical U.S. neighborhood lemonade stand that *children* operate as I said all of this.

"Haaaaah," the middle-aged woman who had voiced this complaint said in disagreement as she fanned herself rapidly with the handout she had been given. "Then before long, we will have to deal with the health department and all that red tape: health cards, rest rooms, and inspections. *Es mejor hacer nada* (It's better to do nothing at all)." The look on my face changed from an encouraging smile to one of shock as I raised my eyebrows and dipped my head as if to say, *Really!? Come again? Are you* ***that*** *unmotivated?* I highly doubted the authorities were going to hassle anyone selling fresh juice from their front porch. In fact, some of the local families did sell ice (water frozen in plastic bags) or *duros* (popsicles that were juice frozen in small plastic bags) out of their homes. After I shared a wide-eyed knowing glance with one of the moderators, he stepped in to reassure this woman that she would probably not be penalized for starting a small business like this. Then, praising my suggestion, he said that these were precisely the low-cost, simple things that tourists *do* enjoy.

Even though this meeting was far less traumatic, I was struck by all of this and again I found myself ruminating, mostly about this woman's depressing sentiment. I also realized that it probably wasn't my place to go to "trainings" such as this one. Even though I had no formal background working in tourism and lacked a college degree, I certainly did have a financial and educational advantage over someone who had hardly ever left the village. I had been exposed to so much by traveling that I actually knew quite a bit more about tourism than I realized, especially if the basics included smiling. Still, I couldn't help but wonder if this statement *es mejor hacer nada* summarized a lot of people's beliefs, and if it was something I shouldn't consider for myself as well. Was I just wasting my time trying to contribute to a community of people who didn't want me here at all? I had vowed to not let living here make me jaded, but I was beginning to feel like I was losing some ground. I reassured myself that not everyone feels this way and was hopeful that at least some of the people from my art group, especially the younger people, were truly interested in and open to an intercultural exchange.

The third meeting I went to, Matt was at the center, and we had become the problem, or at least Matt's new side hustle had.

Matt had convinced his parents to buy a piece of property close to the town beach as an investment. It had an ocean view with a small ramshackle cinderblock building on it. He wanted to create a tourist-friendly bar where people could hang out, relax, and watch a sports game on T.V. while having a few drinks. He came up with this idea, in part, to help Skeech (a good friend and fellow property owner in Joyita) who was currently in the U.S. going through a hard time and wanted to come back to do *something,* he just didn't know what. There wasn't a "gringo bar" in Joyita only the two cantinas in town which were essentially local watering holes. They generally had loud *tipico* music blaring with drunk people sitting around wooden tables on small stools, shouting over the music with the overwhelming smell of piss and beer lingering in the air. Matt's plan included building a small amphitheater for hosting community events and live music. There was definitely a need for this kind of place, but I didn't think *we* needed to be the ones to create it.

For one, I didn't consider owning a bar in alignment with my personal code of ethics, which much like the Buddhist principle of right livelihood was to help, not harm. I did not see selling alcohol as a means to help humanity or the planet. I viewed it as the opposite, actually. Hardly a drinker myself, I had little patience for drunkenness and viewed alcohol as another beast entirely when compared to mind-expanding substances such as marijuana or psychedelics. The latter of these had brought about many spiritual experiences and epiphanies in my life, whereas alcohol (although more socially acceptable) is a depressant, which can not only fuel belligerent behavior and domestic violence but is also responsible for killing millions of people every year. This was a huge reason why I hadn't wanted to serve dinner in our restaurant. Aside from it being way too much work, I didn't want to have to babysit people who were drinking late into the night or feel I was contributing to any belligerent behavior. I was also trying to slow Matt's roll because I couldn't imagine him being away from me, Gabe, or our business any more than he already was with his other "side projects."

More than creating a cool environment, I was sure he was seeing dollar signs, so I argued that I would rather have a greater quality of life with him around, than off trying to make a buck. I also pointed out that no one could serve alcohol in Joyita after 10 p.m. so they would have a very narrow window to make a buck. He assured me that after he gave the building a tiny facelift, it was going to be Skeech's project, and we would just share a percentage of the profits. I dug my heels in as long as I could, but I loved Skeech. He was a huge hippie teddy bear of a guy who was super fun and outgoing. He really was the perfect person to run something like this. The two of them already had *The Dive* picked out as the name. It had a double meaning because it was going to be a dive bar, and they were going to have it covered in murals of underwater scenes people saw while scuba diving in the national park. I began to cast any doubts aside and got on board with their enthusiasm, never suspecting any backlash.

The Dive Bar would be the first foreign owned business that had an actual license to operate as a bar and not as a restaurant where alcohol sales had to be accompanied with food. As Matt began to make structural changes and acquire the liquor license and permits, an oppositional force was gathering strength. We heard rumors that people did not want any more bars or cantinas in the village, but interestingly enough, the people who we were told were being the most vocal about this were also people who enjoyed drinking on a regular basis and were known to be anti-foreigner as well. So, we assumed they didn't want any *foreign* owned bars or cantinas in Joyita. The argument was that for a small town of five hundred residents, there were more than twelve businesses that sold alcohol and consequently contributed to higher incidences of belligerence, violence, and theft. Matt was calling bullshit on this, saying it was obvious that the alcoholism in the community was perpetuated by the two nationally owned cantinas selling fifty cent beers and not the quaint restaurants selling beer and wine with dinner to mainly tourists. This debate, as well as the ridiculousness of the 10 p.m. curfew, began to permeate throughout the village. All of the foreigners agreed that the cantinas were the "cancer" (as they called it) in the village and that as a tourist destination there was a real need for a bar with a nicer atmosphere. Restaurant owners became more vocal about the necessity of serving alcohol to customers after 10 p.m. I understood both perspectives and began to see this issue more as a physical manifestation of the growing pains the town was now experiencing as they were truly beginning to lose their identity and culture to tourism. Still, any and all excitement we *could* have felt about this new endeavor was completely overshadowed by the town's growing disapproval (at least for me).

Now when I walked down the road (which was my number one mode of transportation) I could absolutely tell who was part of the resistance. Lots of the people who used to be warm and friendly towards me were no longer returning my greetings in the street. I was receiving not only silence, but hard stares, which was what everyone called *mal de ojo* or the evil eye. This "stink eye" (as we gringos called it) had a deeper, more insidious meaning than just a dirty look. I had been told that people were casting spells on one another via these cold stares. Supposedly they were actively wishing misfortune, illness, or worse on their enemies. In fact, the local custom was for new mothers to tie a red string bracelet around their baby's wrist to protect them from the *mal de ojo*. I couldn't imagine anyone was actually going around intentionally inflicting ill will on babies, or me for that matter, but I no longer felt comfortable walking down the street in the little paradise we were living in.

"I think you're being too sensitive," Matt told me. "Not everyone is against us, and it's not personal; it's about the bar. They are also worried about the noise factor. This will be short lived. You'll see. Those same people giving you stink eye will eventually be sitting at the bar having a drink." I wasn't so sure, and I gave *him* stink eye because this whole thing really was his fault. I *did* feel one degree of separation from all of this because I knew none of it was my doing and even though Matt was my husband, we were individuals, and I was beginning to see we had very different opinions about things.

The town meeting was called down near The Dive site. It was rumored that the media would be present and people were insisting Matt attend. I was mortified! In the four years we had lived here, we had never seen anything like this. There had already been a few smaller meetings that Matt had blown off, saying he had all the government permits and didn't need to answer to the townspeople.

He was right, but the energy was continuing to grow and people wanted to be heard. They wanted their concerns addressed, and I assumed wanted to feel they still had a say in what happens in their community. Friends from the village (the few I felt we still had) advised him to go, saying this was probably not going to go away until he showed some face. I didn't feel obligated to go to the meeting. In fact, I knew that I probably shouldn't. The criticism and trauma would inevitably stay with me, but I couldn't imagine him going alone. When I did, I envisioned a public stoning, so I decided to go to support him.

When we arrived, we shook hands with the community members who had begun to gather and were introduced to the journalist from one of the national newspapers. We stood in the uncomfortable tension as they waited to see if a television crew would arrive as well. I plastered a dismal smile on my face as I thought *pueblo pequeño infierno grande* which means small town big hell and was a popular phrase in Joyita. After about thirty minutes of small talk and awkwardness it was decided that the press was good enough and the meeting officially began. They started by painting a picture of the alcoholism that was quite prevalent in the village. They described fights in the street, how drinking attributes to poverty because sadly, rather than spending money on food for their families, some people spend all their money in the bars, and how the worst of the worst, the few men who were *extreme* alcoholics, could be seen passed out on the side of the road on any given day. I agreed. All of this was absolutely true.

The main spokesman and known village provocateur went on to dramatically explain the collective concern. "We do not need more businesses fueling the fire of *alcoholismo*. It is the foreigners that are bringing alcohol and drugs to our community and corrupting our youth." *Ohhhh hell no*, I thought, feeling my feathers beginning to ruffle. He went on to provide more evidence of this "foreign corruption" reminding the large crowd that had now gathered that there had been foreigners who live in *their* community arrested for drugs. I was fuming now. Those foreigners were our good friends, one of whom had spent three months in jail for a couple of joints that he would smoke in the privacy of his own home! None of these people were corrupting the youth!

After addiction, he moved into the problem of noise, pointing out that there are a number of local homes that had school aged children nearby and then summarized with, "This is still a community, not a party destination," leaning towards Matt and looking him in the eyes. "We will now allow Señor Mateo to speak about this *cantina* he is planning on opening. What do you have to say in respect to these valid concerns from the community Señor Mateo?" I prayed that Matt's basic Spanish would be enough to express himself and this wasn't when the stones would come out.

He opened on the defensive saying he was not doing anything wrong or illegal (*oh oh, not good,* I thought) and that he wasn't opening a cantina (*okay*). But as he tried to explain that the local alcoholics were not going to be his clientele, that's not what it sounded like in his elementary Spanish. It came across more like, "I don't want these people as clients," causing an offended type of stirring in the crowd to begin. When he tried to make his point by saying he planned on charging $2 for a beer and $4 for a glass of wine to tourists, disapproval spread like wildfire. *"No one will pay that!"* and *"You just want to make money!"* were amongst the many comments being expressed simultaneously. Eventually things simmered down enough for the local arbitrator to interrupt. "So, you are not opening a cantina Señor Mateo? Are you opening a *bar* or a *restaurant*?" I knew that Skeech and Matt were only planning on serving peanuts, but at that moment he must have decided peanuts were the qualifying factor for a restaurant, or to change their business plan.

"Yes. We are planning on opening a restaurant."

"Ah, so this establishment that you and Señor Eskeesh are opening will be serving food? Because I was told it is a bar and that you have a liquor license. And where is Señor Eskeesh? Is he here in the *pueblo*?" Sounding like a town appointed judge, he continued his line of questioning.

"Yes, we will be serving food and no, Skeech is not in Panamá now. He is in *Los Estados Unidos*."

"Okay, well we were under the impression that this was going to be a bar. This is good news, right?" He asked the crowd of familiar faces, opening the meeting to general commentary. A woman who we were friends with, and Matt was always joking around with spoke. "You all know that my house is right here, really close, and I'm worried about the noise! My kids are in school, and they need to get a good night's sleep." This led to another woman yelling about her children having to walk by the cantina in the morning on their way to school while they played pornographic movies with both the audio and the picture loud and clear on the television set that they could see. Clearly angry, she wanted to know how this could be going on if legally the cantinas must have a privacy wall or screen up so that minors cannot see inside. She was demanding that the cantina be forced to comply with this. More women rallied, shaking their fingers at the arbitrator and the journalist telling them they needed to make this public. For once I was grateful that a meeting was completely off the rails.

The bottom line was they didn't want any more foreign owned businesses in Joyita, but I knew this was impossible. I sympathized; I totally did. As hypocritical as it was, I didn't want Joyita to be overrun by tourism either, but seventy percent of the town had already been sold to foreigners. It was legal for foreigners to purchase property and to own businesses *everywhere* in the country. Joyita was not going to be the exception to this rule. The government was giving tax incentives for foreign investment in the tourism sector, *wanting* the development. Having grown up in the U.S. and traveled, I knew that change was happening everywhere in the world, and it was inevitable. There would be no going back. It was unrealistic to think that Joyita would go backwards while the rest of the world continued to move forward at such a fast pace towards globalization.

From there, it escalated to wild speculation and downright lies about us not paying social security for our employees and that Matt had said he was going to have the school moved up the road to put in a bar or *discoteca* across the street from us instead. I just shook my head, finally speaking to defend myself as well. I said none of this was true. We did indeed pay social security, and we did not own, could not move, nor did we want to move the school. I could not see this getting any better. Feeling emotionally drained and that nothing more could or should be said, I told Matt I thought we should just go. So after a short interview with the journalist, hand in hand, we walked home.

"Well, that went all right," he said happily as we walked up the hill.

"What!? That was one of the worst experiences of my life! There was a town meeting held ***against*** *us! I don't want everyone in the village hating me!"*

"Oh, it wasn't against us personally and everyone was happy that I said it would be a restaurant. Problem solved. Now I just need to tell Skeech we have to serve food. That'll be better actually." I was glad he was so optimistic because I could not see the bright side to any of this.

As we continued walking up the street, Guapo greeted us with his usual, "*Vecino*" (neighbor), but then vocalized my perspective by adding empathetically, "oh, vecino, they cooked you down there." Shaking his head sadly he said he had just got back from fishing but couldn't bring himself to watch. Appreciating his support, I thought, well, at least Matt is right, and the *entire* village isn't against us, letting in a little silver lining of my own.

The next day, the group from the meeting was on the front page of the newspaper holding banners that we hadn't seen there which read, "NO MÁS BARES, NO MÁS RESTAURANTES, NO MÁS ALCOHOLISMO." The article went on to explain the reason for yesterday's protest was to fight against the opening of a new cantina, which had received both the business and liquor license from national and local authorities. It said that the result of yesterday's demonstration was that the community had decided the authorities could no longer grant any more permits for cantinas.

Errrr impossible, I thought. It was the other way around. It's the authorities that grant permits not the community telling the authorities what they can and cannot do. Though, I had to hand it to them for taking the law into their own hands. It just sucked that it was aimed at us.

In the end, Matt was right. Skeech arrived the next week and started spending time down at The Dive. He was cleaning, stocking the shelves, shaking hands, handing out free beers, and making friends. Pretty soon, the door was open, and some of the same people who were vocal at the meeting were there on a bar stool hitting on tourist women. Friends got together there regularly for goodbye parties or to celebrate birthdays, and Skeech and Matt threw an epic New Year's bash that locals, foreigners, and tourists attended. Slowly but surely the stink eye was replaced with *saludos* (greetings) again, but now I was weary not knowing if I should take anything at face value here anymore. I was beginning to get the feeling that under the surface we would probably never be accepted. And ironically, the *alcoholismo* that everyone had fought so hard against was making its way into Matt's, and therefore *my* life as well.

Chapter 17

We're not on Vacation

Prior to The Dive, Matt had slowly been working his way towards alcoholism. When he was in and around La Buena Vida, he would start drinking pre-lunch having a "red beer," which was a beer with tomato juice. Then another (or two) with lunch, a few prior to dinner, with dinner, and possibly after. On any given day he was having 6-10 drinks. That was if there wasn't a game or a party going on. If there was some sort of cause for celebration, he'd have 12-20 drinks in a day, and then he was no longer a normally functioning human being.

When we were living in Alaska, Matt and I would have an occasional social drink with dinner, but usually only if we went out or were entertaining. We never drank at home just the two of us, so this was entirely new behavior. This was still pre-cellphones (in the village), so we had no way of getting in touch with one another. He would tell me he was, "going to watch the game," meaning down at The Dive, which if it started at 7 p.m., I'd assume he would be finished by 10, but I'd wake up at midnight and he wouldn't be back. I'd feel the bed alongside of me again at 2 a.m., and he still wasn't there. I'd go from worried, to angry, to the point of not being able to sleep. This made me even more angry, because I am someone who does not function well on little sleep, and I was still getting up at 5:45 *every* morning to open the restaurant.

This went on to varying degrees for nearly a year. I'd bitch, lecture, cry and complain after every episode, and then he'd refrain for a few weeks, a month, or two, and then this cycle would continue. But it climaxed on New Years of 2011. We (Matt mostly) had begun to organize an annual river float on New Year's Day and friends were going to meet at our place at 9 a.m. to caravan together. There was a big party at The Dive with our German friend DJing, but shortly after midnight, I went home to get some rest because I would be organizing and packing the food and water for the twenty-some people we expected to attend. I kissed Matt goodbye, and he reassured me that he was going to help Skeech clean up and would be home shortly. Matt was not home when I woke up at 2 a.m., nor at 4 a.m. When he finally came home at 6 a.m. barely able to walk, I couldn't believe it! *How did he expect to be up and running to help me to get ready in another 2 hours!?* He wasn't. He slept right through the first wave of excited river rafters who hadn't gone out partying at all and were fully packed and ready to go. They were very disappointed as I spoke to them, and they opted out of waiting around all morning to see if anyone was going to be coherent enough later to make this excursion actually happen. As embarrassing as this was, I knew none of it was my fault. I apologized in this way, keeping my cool and fully empathizing by saying that I was up and ready to go, too. But inside, my blood was boiling. I was angry and disappointed as well, and I knew this was *not okay*. Something had to change!

When everyone finally did rally to go river rafting, it was about 12 noon, and we had an excellent time. But another one of my meltdowns was just on a snooze waiting for a more appropriate time to address Matt's drinking problem once again.

"Do you even think you have a problem?" I asked him, pointing out that his drinking was indeed affecting other people, mainly me, but in the case of this excursion, the people who he had disappointed that were all set to participate. "I think you have an addictive personality in general. Everything you do is in full force. Do you realize that you're not actually on vacation!?" I wanted to know. He remained mostly silent as I pointed out the fact that in a transient tourist town, it is always someone's first night or last night, and that there will always be a reason to party. "And celebrating is one thing, but to drink yourself into a stupor so that you cannot even walk is another. It's super unhealthy."

"You're right. I'm sorry."

"So, what can be done to change?"

"I don't know, I'll change."

"How? I mean, I know I shouldn't force someone to change, but you are not the person I first met. This is not the person I married. *You've changed*, and I'd like to see how I can get my husband back."

I needed to know the actions he planned on taking to change. We needed some ground rules and to establish what was going to be acceptable and not acceptable from this point forward. I was getting nothing from him, so I said the only thing that came to my mind. "Maybe we need to have a written agreement where some ground rules are established so there is absolutely no gray area. So that you don't say, 'I'm going to watch a game,' and then come home completely inebriated six hours later. What if *I* did that? What if I told you I'm going out to dinner with my girlfriends, and then I didn't come home at all and was out all night long? Is that okay with you?"

"No."

"So, what's a reasonable hour to come home? And when is it an appropriate occasion to stay out later? For me, a basketball game is not a good enough reason to stay out all night. A birthday or a bachelor party is a special occasion that for me would be acceptable to know you were going to be home late. I'm not being completely unreasonable here Matt."

"I know," he said, continuing to look down and avoid eye contact with me.

"So could you be home by 10 p.m. if we haven't previously discussed you staying out late for a special occasion? That could be our agreement? Out of respect for me and my need to get a good night's sleep in order to open the restaurant early in the morning, you can agree to be home by 10 p.m.?"

"Yes."

So, with my blood still boiling, I put it in writing and asked him to sign the terms of our new agreement. I made it clear that this was *my* last stitch effort. It was okay if he wanted to hang out at the bar or occasionally have a special late night out with the guys, but if he couldn't honor the agreement, I was done, and there would need to be a much larger shift. Writing a contractual agreement for my husband to sign that essentially gave him a curfew of 10 p.m. definitely seemed strange, but I didn't know what else we could do. It wasn't okay for him to not come home all night long, and now I had written proof that he recognized it was an issue. If and when it happened again, I had evidence of my expectations clearly in writing and he had agreed to them. So in my mind, I was back to waiting and hoping again, giving him one more chance to find more self-discipline when it came to his drinking.

Things were going smoothly, and Matt was respecting our agreement until some of our best friends arrived from Alaska after buying Guapo's house next door and there was reason for more celebration. They were both teachers on Kodiak Island and had three boys who were in and around the same age as Gabe, so it was great to have them close by for a few weeks during their summer break. They hung with us in the restaurant everyday between beach excursions with the kids and landscaping projects at their new place. I was going to drive them back to Panama City for their return flight and for the first time ever (in over two years running the restaurant), I asked Matt to open it for me and handle things while I was away. But he never came home that night.

At two in the morning, when I woke up and he wasn't there, I was pissed! The anger and adrenaline I had pulsing through my veins didn't allow me to sleep. I tossed and turned until four a.m. furious that this was the *one time* I had asked him to manage the restaurant. I had such a long day and drive ahead of me that I really wanted and *needed* to get a good night's sleep so that I could be at my best. I was so furious I decided I was not going to let him sleep in the bed with me when he did get home because there was no way I could sleep next to him. I may have drifted off momentarily, but I awoke to the sound of him trying and failing to open the front door and then peeing right alongside the entrance to the house.

I threw the front door open to find him barely able to stand, much less walk. I told him to sleep on the couch or in one of the hotel rooms. "You have to open the restaurant in an hour," I told him, knowing that would not be possible. He swayed in large circles as he stood in one place letting this sink in, and then grabbed the car keys off the bar as if he was going to drive away. I held his shoulders asking, "Where are you going? You cannot drive like this, and I need the car to take Erin and Avery to the airport."

"Lemmmme go, you said I can't stay here."

We began to get into a physical standoff where I was able to hold him back because he was so inebriated. But I couldn't let go, and I couldn't convince him to just sleep on the couch or in a cabana. "No, I'm leaving if you don't want me to sleep with you," he said. I tried pulling the keys out of his hands, and they ended up flying across the room. I ran to the window and shouted for our friends to come while he was distracted, screaming both of their names, and then back to constrain Matt as he made his way to the front door, keys in hand. I had never been in a domestic dispute like this in my life, and I had certainly never involved other people in drunken and disorderly conduct, but here we were with his son sleeping in the same room throughout all of this.

Erin arrived and brought me up to speed by telling me that even though he had been at the bar with Matt the entire time, he was not drinking top shelf tequila like Matt and Skeech had been, so he was totally coherent. "I just want to go to sleep, bro," Matt told him, "but she won't let me."

"I don't want to sleep next to him like this," I further explained. "and now he thinks he is going to drive somewhere."

"Dude, just lay down and go to bed," Erin said.

"She won't let me."

"I don't want him in bed next to me, I'm too pissed off, and he stinks!"

"I get it, but Michelle, he's just going to pass out, and then this will all be over. Just let him lay down, and he'll be out." *Over for him*, I thought, but not for *me*, knowing I wouldn't be able to sleep, and *I* would have to open the restaurant in less than an hour. Erin walked Matt to the bed and let him lay down, but I was seething about his drinking and how unfair it was that I had been managing the restaurant for over two years and the one time I was counting on him, he really let me down. We were supposed to be a team, and I had to be able to rely on my partner. This was absolutely unacceptable!

After alternating between fuming on the couch and lying next to Matt in bed, now snoring, I went and opened the restaurant for the girls, and then went straight back to bed managing to sleep another hour or so before getting up and having breakfast with our friends and the kids. Matt got out of bed somehow to say goodbye to them before we left, but I wasn't talking to him, nope. We would have to have a long talk when I got back because I refused to be in such an unhealthy relationship.

Upon my return, my anger had *not* subsided. In fact, having a full day in the car with friends to discuss it and then a full day driving home by myself, it had bubbled up and was now boiling over. For the first time, Matt was now subject to hearing just how pissed off I was while he was sober; how I felt I was unable to rely on him and how much his drinking affected *my* sleep and therefore *my* health. "Something has to change," I told him, finishing my rant by saying, "I came here with a backpack, and I will leave here with a backpack. And I am dead fucking serious. I will walk away from all of this and start over. I don't fucking care about any of it. I'm not going to live like this."

Tears filled his eyes as he told me, "I promise babe, I'll change. You'll see," but at this point, I figured the change would have to be me leaving. He had tried moderation, and that was *not* working.

"You have to," I said, skeptically wondering if anything could be done on his part, if I should even stick around to witness this change, or if I should just leave and come back if he did indeed change.

"*How* are you going to change?" I needed to know.

"I don't know, I'll quit drinking."

"You're going to quit drinking *cold turkey*?"

"Yes."

This seemed extreme to me and was *not* what I was expecting to hear. Drinking had become a huge part of who he was and what he and his friends *did*. He owned a bar for God's sake! I had imagined that our change would be that he would only drink on special occasions, or that I would pack my bags and leave. But in all honesty, leaving wasn't what I wanted, and it didn't seem fair that *I* should be the one to leave.

"Ok, well, I'm serious, I told him. This *cannot* happen again and *you're* the one saying you are going to quit drinking completely. You know that's not going to be easy, right? You're sure that's what you want to do?

"Babe, you're the most important thing I have in my life. You and Gabe. After that, nothing else matters. I'm going to change. I'm going to prove that you can count on me. You'll see."

"All right," I said, completely doubting he could quit cold turkey and thinking he was just setting himself up for failure. In my mind, the change he needed to make should be more realistic, but I knew that drinking less only worked until he drank more again. Maybe this was the best possible decision. If he did fail, I didn't know what my next step would be. I mentally explored my options. Maybe it would depend on just how badly he messed up. Maybe I'd go live with my parents in Florida and do massage therapy until I saved enough money to start over on my own again or until he sold La Buena Vida and was able to pay me my half of our investment here. Maybe leaving Panamá would be the only wake-up call that actually inspired change. I resolved to buckle my skeptical seat belt and see what would happen, preparing for the turbulent winds of change ahead.

Chapter 18

Romanticizing the Stone

I was beginning to realize that not only had I completely romanticized our life together in "tropical paradise," I had romanticized living amongst poverty as well. As a cute little tourist girl, spending my money, of course I had felt accepted and welcome as I traveled throughout the tropics. As a backpacker, if I ever thought about local attitudes toward foreigners, my raging case of tourist denial and the fact that I had been camping on the beach or selling jewelry on the street, led me to believe that I was somehow different and more like the locals. While traveling, I had loved "experiencing" other cultures, but now I began to ask myself if we can truly be having a cultural experience if we are merely *witnessing* another culture. I had been enchanted by the Kichwa people in Ecuador washing their clothes in the river, but I didn't have to carry my clothes to the river to wash them and wait for hours as they sundried on the rocks. I never had to wash my clothes in a river, and I never stopped to ask myself what that must mean for them. It was picturesque for me at that moment, but I had my private room with a hot shower and laundry service to go back to.

Similarly, I could see that even though I was interacting with Panamanian culture every day, my experience living here was a completely different reality from the local families that we lived amongst. Along with poverty and alcoholism, I knew that sexual and physical abuse was generally tolerated here. I knew that people were struggling to clothe and feed themselves. The lack of amenities in Joyita that we viewed as charming was coming from a place of over-excess that we still had access to in the U.S. Plus, we had a car and a budget that allowed us to zip into town to buy what we needed, when we needed it. Taking the bus into Santiago was almost twice as long as going by car, and cost nearly a days' wage, which was about $13. Though I wasn't experiencing this first hand, I was witnessing it, and it touched me deeply, especially when as a business owner, I realized that I may now be acting as "the oppressor."

I had left the U.S. because I didn't want to participate in an oppressive system I didn't believe in. It had always been my intention to be part of the community here and somehow "give back." That became even more important to me as I realized that we were now capitalists benefitting from the cheap price of land and labor. Before coming here, I had never really looked that far ahead to consider the real implications and impact of living and working in a place like Joyita. I had planned on living a simpler lifestyle of doing massage without any employees. Now that we were here doing business on a larger scale, I was feeling torn as I witnessed my own shift in values. I was holding myself, our business, and our employees to high standards. As I preached the importance of punctuality, attendance, working together as a team, and taking initiative, I knew that instilling American ideals in our minimum wage workers was necessary if we wanted our business to operate smoothly. But I also knew that I was now a missionary propagating cultural change which was a far cry from the reason I had intended to come here: to embrace and be part of the local culture.

To reconcile this, I tried my best as a boss to be fair and kind. Even though I loved our employees, I knew that I couldn't be best friends with them, or I *would* get taken advantage of. As it turned out, McDonald's warning of, "give them an inch and they'll take a mile" *did* have some validity. Not with everyone, but generosity was often interpreted as weakness and as an endless fountain. Being an employer became a diplomatic dance of sorts as I looked for ways to be firm, but also respectful, giving everyone grace as I reminded myself that this morality, and even the tasks themselves, were brand new to most. I told myself it was hard for someone to know how to clean a bathroom if they didn't have a toilet and still used an outhouse at home. I wanted our employees to be able to get ahead financially and improve their living situations which I knew translated to "more is better" and was an ideology I had been resisting my entire adult life. I rationalized this because obviously I wasn't talking about fancy sports cars, entertainment systems, or sail boats. It would have just been nice to see them have indoor plumbing, or in the very least, a cinderblock home and not a bamboo shack. I didn't know how that would be possible on minimum wage, and I began to carry the weight of this on my shoulders, feeling an even greater need to contribute where I could.

I saw that stress, the pressure to be more productive and responsible, or the need to learn English weren't necessarily cultural changes everyone was open to. But there was some receptivity when it came to improving education, donating food and clothing, and the garbage issue in town, so I began to focus my community service in these areas. As much as I would have liked to help the local children who were going hungry or struggling in abusive households, the kids who had it the worse at home *were* the worst. The same day we fed a ten-year-old-boy a peanut butter sandwich at the bar while we helped him to write his name *(yes, at ten years old!)* and with simple math, I caught him behind the bar that night with the remote control to the speaker in his hand. The adolescent we took to the pizzeria one night, who Matt had been teaching to play basketball, is the only person in the village who has ever broke into our home (the next week). We weren't the only ones this happened to. It seemed by opening your heart and your home to a few children in particular (and in a small town like this we all knew who they were), you would only be allowing yourself to be taken advantage of. While offering a hungry child a plate of food, they were "casing the joint" to come back later and steal from you. Knowing we couldn't help some of the children who were most in need, Matt instead got involved with forming a local kid's baseball league together with Fausti who coached The Joyita team. Matt transported them to away games and helped to get lots of equipment donated by friends and family coming from the U.S, not just for the local team, but for some of the poorer neighboring villages as well.

Along with the local art workshops, I became active in The Joyita Chamber of Tourism and with the community recycle center that they opened. I took on managing the recycle center and began teaching environmental education once a week at the school. I started with the basics; talking about different ways to responsibly handle our garbage at home and the effects of not keeping it contained and allowing rubbish to be in streets, streams, and then eventually the ocean. After each lesson we would make a fun recycled art project. The kids were incentivized to bring recycling to the school, which I bribed them to do by creating charts and offering prizes. There were town and beach cleanups involved in the program, and it was amazing to eventually see the kids hauling large garbage bags of recycled plastic bottles that they collected from the beach on their own time to the school. Some of the parents were very supportive, but the English expression "no good deed goes unpunished" *did* directly translate here. And with everything I did, there always seemed to be finger pointers and naysayers. When I managed to get speed bumps installed in front of the school because the cars, especially the huge eighteen-wheeler delivery trucks, drove way too fast through the village just honking at the kids to get out of the way, people said we only did that so traffic would have to slow down and look at our business. Foreign community members who never physically helped with the recycle program had lots of suggestions as to how I could do things "better." I told myself to just keep my head down and continue because these were the things that I was passionate about; giving back, the kids, art, the environment, and recycling. Plus, I could see it *was* making a difference. Some of the kids would stop me on the street, give me hugs, and ask when we were doing another beach cleanup. I'd exude tons of positivity as I shared with them how exciting it was that they could go and clean the beach anytime they wanted *on their own* which to me seemed like a huge revelation. This would always lead to sideways glances and a, "Ohhhhh Míchel, come on," you-know-what-we-mean, we want to do it together with *you*, kind of response.

Matt was a few months into not drinking, and it was going reasonably well. It was obvious that he had transferred all of his addictive-energy into working full force, and it was amazing how much more productive he was now without taking beer breaks before, during, and after lunch. When he was at La Buena Vida, he was either laying down the law, joking, or both with the employees. He and Fausti had a running joke that really highlighted our cultural differences. Every day as Fausti was leaving work in the afternoon we would thank him and say, "*Gracias*, see you tomorrow," to which his response was usually, "*Si Dios quiere*," which literally means if God wants, but translates more to "God willing." Matt would then reply, "Yes, God *does* want you to come to work tomorrow," which would always crack Fausti up. He would shake his head and laughing respond, "*Esso Mateo* (Oh Matt), you can't know God's will." Seeing the greater picture, he'd explain to Matt that everything is in God's hands, and that we can't possibly know what tomorrow will bring. "I could become sick or something else may come up that requires my attention and keeps me from coming to work, *verdad*?" Of course, this *was* true, but from our cultural perspective, it seemed a bit melodramatic to be used in this sense *every day,* and Matt always remained adamant that God *did* want him to come to work. Fausti would laugh in disbelief of Matt's sacrilege and begin to preach another widely used Panamanian phrase, *Dios primero* (God first). This was a beautiful sentiment about putting God first in our lives, and it was also used as a general disclaimer for anything that might happen like, "*God first* the MRI machine will be working if you drive three hours one way to come to this appointment." And though it was clear that Matt was now putting *his* work (not God, La Buena Vida, or even me) first, I was so immersed in life itself, that I hadn't realized just how much my free-spirited nature and my *own* trust in God or the Universe had changed. The old Miller in me had been completely down with the openness of "God willing" and putting him/her first. In the past I had trusted that if something was meant to be, that God / The Universe would find a way. Now when I heard 'God willing,' it felt good in that it was acknowledging God was overseeing a greater plan for us, which some deep part of me knew I had become disconnected from. But this phrase also lacked the personal power, free will, and motivation that I had stepped into out of necessity, to keep everything in our lives running smoothly. God willing felt indifferent to me now; like "throwing your hands in the air and wavin' 'em like you just don't care."[22] The new hotel and restaurant owner me felt we needed to take action in order to ensure God's will happened.

It felt as if *I*, not God, was dedicated to overseeing *everything* at La Buena Vida. The reservations, website, check-ins, check-outs, restaurant inventory, lunch specials, maintenance, employee scheduling, tasks, accounting, and payroll. And though I did wish we could pay them more, after paying for their social security, a month of paid vacation, and an additional month's salary every year (which was what we were legally required to pay everyone) multiplied by six employees, it was nearly impossible. The girls in the restaurant earned more with tips, and we loaned our long-term employees money to finance their home improvement projects or to buy larger

---

[22] Rock Master Scott & The Dynamic Three, "The Roof is on Fire," A-side single on *The Roof is on Fire*, Reality/Fantasy, 1985, vinyl

appliances when we could. But the thought that I could and should be doing more continued to weigh on me regularly, and I had a huge sense of guilt when I thought about us "getting ahead," building a bigger house for ourselves, or going on vacation while our employees continued to live in very basic conditions.

Matt did not share my perspective. He was of the opinion that by giving people work, we were giving them opportunity. He was always telling me that I wasn't charging enough for food in the restaurant and routinely pointed out that we still weren't paying ourselves a paycheck and as self-employed people we had no pension to rely on later in life. Now in his forties, he was worried about our financial future and building a proper house for ourselves above the hotel grounds. We had both drawn up some ideas for our house on the hill, but we couldn't come to an agreement. My plan was a two story, two bedroom, two bath. Matt's included a pool, a huge man cave, and other things that I *never* wanted and thought were unjustifiable living amongst such poverty. I began to question how much is enough, and when people should begin to allow their cup to overflow to help others. His argument was that we were still living in a six hundred square foot *studio* within the hotel which gave us no reprieve from our business. Gabe was ten now and he wanted him (and us) to have his own room and privacy. I got it, but I also saw that once we had our nice big house with the ocean view, that probably wouldn't be enough either, that there would always be something else important to spend on for ourselves.

"Michelle, you just gave our employees all the old hotel sheets and restaurant dishes. We can't give everything we own away, or we will never have anything either."

I knew this was true, but the amount he was working, the amount we were *both* working (twelve to fourteen hour days) was more than we had worked in the U.S. And for me, it was getting to be ridiculous, especially because Matt had so many other side hustles going that all of the day to day operations at La Buena Vida had fallen on me. I was adamant that I came here for quality of life, not *quantity*, and that we were working so hard we didn't need to worry about money, it would come. I had come a long way from wanting to be a bag lady when I grew up, but for me, a big house and a swimming pool was *not* part of the dream. I had come here to live a simple lifestyle, to live closer to nature, and to value people over profit.

Matt clearly upset, countered with, "Look around. In order to get ahead here people have to hustle! Nearly every foreigner has two or three things they do to make money because it's one thing to just live, *tranquilo* getting by, but it's another thing to earn enough money for us to leave and go back to the U.S. or for me to pay child support! And you say you still want to travel. You talk about going to India. I want to make that happen for us, for you!" This all rang true to me and for the first time I saw the role I was playing in Matt's financial drive. But India was one thing; a big fancy house with a pool was another. I wanted to live somewhere in between our first world upbringing and the third world living conditions that surrounded us.

The conversation about our future house had become a stalemate and Matt continued to entertain each and every job offer that came his way. The Dive had been short lived and now he had moved on to considering importing roofing from China or possibly overseeing the construction of a huge housing development 300 kilometers away. He talked about creating an entire town somewhere else, or "wifi-ing" the community by bringing high speed Internet to Joyita. He was open to each and every opportunity that was presented to him. Even though this had always been my attitude towards life in the past, it wasn't now, not when it came to entertaining business ideas that for me lacked conscientiousness or would take him further away from helping me with what we had created together.

Because Matt was adventurous and had been willing to set out with me to create an unconventional lifestyle, I had just assumed he had been motivated by the same ideals and values that I was. But I was beginning to realize that maybe that wasn't the case. I had wanted to relocate to live amongst another culture and have a more relaxed lifestyle. I had been allowing my heart to guide me, but economic opportunity seemed to be what was guiding Matt. It was also becoming apparent to me that Matt was used to a higher standard of living and travel than I was. I had grown up camping, and he had grown up vacationing in hotels, his family making an annual pilgrimage to Baltimore to eat blue crabs, and flying to see the final four basketball games every March. He had bought sports cars for himself in his twenties, whereas I had been content just sleeping in my van. Even though we both loved each other very much, it felt like our values were so different that we were becoming disconnected from one another and our original goal (or what *I thought* was our original goal) for being here together.

Matt's solution for me feeling overworked and wanting his help was, "So don't work so much. I see you washing dishes and cleaning rooms while the girls have ass time. You don't need to be doing those things. You need to delegate." "Ass time" was what he called it when the restaurant staff (or any staff for that matter) took a break and was sitting on their asses. Though it was true, I would occasionally jump in and help them to do their jobs, it was rare that they were actually sitting on their asses while I was doing these things. And I had to cover one day a week for the waitress, and each cook, and occasionally clean rooms too if the cleaning staff didn't show up. In his mind, our time was more valuable than menial jobs like cleaning toilets when I had administrative tasks that also had to be done. But for me, I knew that shit wouldn't get done or food wouldn't be served in a reasonable time frame if I didn't jump in, and our reputation was on the line. Plus, I wanted to show the employees that we were one and the same, and that I wasn't "above" doing any type of work. Matt thought that was stupid and only perpetuated ass time saying, "You should have the girls do it." But I didn't want to feel like a total capitalist tyrant boss overworking our employees by sending them in circles to clean rooms if their job was in the restaurant, especially for $2 an hour.

All of this became our ongoing yin and yang dynamic. I was being driven by virtues to be of service, and when it came to our finances, I wanted to go with the flow, allow, and trust the rest would come. Matt was brutally honest, practical, and driven financially. He was chasing a future for us outside of La Buena Vida and "making shit happen," but it was *too much shit* in my opinion. Friend's marveled at our differences saying we made such a good team and really complemented one another, but on the inside of this yin and yang, we were knocking the same pinball around and around in the circle, making it impossible for us to move forward.

With neither of us willing or able to shift our perspectives around our future home or how to operate our business, we began to look for other solutions outside of ourselves. In the past we had entertained the idea of having regular international volunteers like our German friends did, but I didn't like the idea of high turnover. I felt like it would take more effort on my part than it was worth to constantly be training new arrivals who could only stay on a tourist visa for three months. Training a local staff member to work in the reception or oversee the restaurant seemed far more sustainable, but we were yet to find someone who spoke fluent English and was responsible. "Maybe we should hire a manager." Matt suggested. "It would be another expense, but *they* could give the girls ass time and give you more quality of life. That would give me more freedom to make money outside of our business." This became the temporary solution that we focused on. The medicine to alleviate the symptoms but not treat the underlying problem or disconnect.

Chapter 19

The Magic?

We were receiving national tourists as well as guests from all over the world which seemed to come in cycles: asshole, asshole, assholes x 10, cool people, repeat. I was becoming dizzy; losing myself to a long string of demanding and draining guests and then finally some real stars would come through. The stars were people who loved our artwork, the food in the restaurant, and who were grateful that Joyita was still an authentic destination *without* any large development. They'd arrive open for adventure and be rewarded with rainbows and whale sharks. The assholes were the guests that stayed in their rooms staring at the spinning wheel of doom (with the slow wifi that we now had) on their computer screen and complained about the lack of *everything*. So in my mind, of course they weren't going to notice any rainbows or the kids clip clopping along in the street pretending they are horses by walking on coconut halves they had on strings between their toes. We had only been in business for four and a half years now, but I was already tired. And I was surprised to find myself becoming jaded, not from the local culture, but from working in tourism. I had come to dread trying to manage tourist's expectations, and without realizing it, instead of my endless optimism of the past, I was always anticipating the worst and assumed customers were going to be difficult. And something I had never imagined while daydreaming about working in tourism was just how repetitive it actually is.

Tourism is repetitive in that you answer the same superficial questions day after day, both personal and about the area or the country in general. "Where are you from?" "How long have you lived here?" And my personal favorite, "Do you love it here?" Then there were the questions that were impossible to answer: *'Do you know how long it is supposed to rain for"* and *"when will the electricity come back?"* With no reliable weather source and power outages that typically lasted 4-16 hours, it was becoming increasingly more difficult to not say, 'I have no fucking idea." We tried to be proactive keeping tourists at arms-length while keeping a sense of humor. I drew the art for Matt to weld a new full-length door for the restaurant to create more of an obvious boundary when we were closed. We usually cooked and ate dinner in the restaurant after hours, and prior to the door, we had a waist high gate that people would just step over to talk to us when they saw us inside. As Matt installed the door, he tested it from the outside sending his arm and torso through the metal bars under the large driftwood CLOSED sign. He reached through the open surfboard and wave designs saying, "Hello, hello, is the restaurant closed? Can we use the wifi? I have a few questions."

My cousin had been temporarily managing the restaurant, but he couldn't answer all of people's questions, especially giving travel recommendations for other destinations. So to alleviate some of my suffering, I wrote a book! My first one. It was entitled "Q & A with M & M." There was one in every room, and one on the giant mosaic surfboard coffee table I had made in the restaurant. I was happy to answer a question or two for someone, but if anyone became really inquisitive, I would kindly refer them to the book. I had begun to delegate a bit more, but my days were still spent in the hotel reception or running around in circles putting out continual fires. I'd be flipping breakers, rebooting the Internet, trying to fix hot water heaters, orchestrating unclogging toilets, exterminating ants; it was endless!

One day a cute young hippie girl came walking into the restaurant. She was dressed in a white tank top and baggy khaki shorts and adorned with strands of beads on her ankles, wrists and neck. She shook my hand and then proceeded to ask me if she and her boyfriend could set up their tent. She motioned to him standing in our parking lot with their backpacks, waving and smiling, and then to the space in our front yard where the hut had once stood. She said they could pay me for the use of a bathroom, showers, and a kitchen, but not having any public facilities like that, I let out an uncomfortable laugh. "Noooo, sorry," I said. "We don't have camping facilities."

"But you must have bathrooms in your restaurant," her eyes darted around, presumably looking for restrooms, "and a kitchen, that maybe we could use?" The thought of them assuming they could use our restaurant kitchen to cook their food produced slightly more awkward laughter on my part. The look on this girl's face visibly changed from hopeful to one of disappointment, and then disapproval which I imagined was her perceiving me as uppity and unsympathetic to her cause. At that moment, I saw myself in this girl. The girl I once was fifteen years ago, moving about the world camping and traveling as a wide-eyed hippie backpacker. I imagined my younger self looking at modern day me through her eyes, and I knew that the Miller in me would have thought I was a cold hearted, rich bitch unwilling to share my abundance of resources.

I continued our conversation more gently asking if they had just arrived, and then explained that there were plenty of other places that do offer camping, even right on the beach or in front of the surf wave. But still, this interaction had shaken me up. That afternoon as I went on a walk (something that I *needed* to do for myself every few days as a way to destress and have a bit of alone time) I tried to see Playa Joyita through the eyes of a recently arrived tourist or through the perspective of my twenty-year-old self. I was looking for magic. Magic that I knew still existed here, but I was no longer seeing for myself. I looked at the colorful hot pink and turquoise homes, at the people I passed and greeted on horseback, and at a flock of green parrots flying by. When I got to the beach, I realized I hadn't been there in over a month, and I couldn't remember the last time I had swam in the ocean! I saw the beachfront camping that could be had for $5 per person and knew this must be a huge source of joy for young visitors, but it was all just normal to me. As I continued walking, the song "The Thrill is Gone," played in my head, and I asked myself when was the last time I got really excited about something here?[23] When was the last time I noticed a synchronicity? A coincidence? There was no

[23] Originally composed by Ray Henderson with lyrics by Lew Brown, "The Thrill is Gone," was first sung by Everett Marshall in Broadway revue *George White's Scandal* in 1931, and would later be performed by B.B. King, Stevie Wonder, Jerry Garcia and many more.

novelty in Joyita for me anymore. And somehow, I had turned into this "rich woman" with the fancy place that didn't let people camp on her property. I had lost myself or who I *was* in everything that I had allowed to become me: our business, working long hours, the annoyance of disgruntled guests.

"Of course, these people think this place is fucking magical," Hippie Matthew told me as I brooded aloud. "They're on fucking vacation, and you guys are over here grinding it out in the trenches working eighteen hours a day, man! I don't know how you do it." I was beginning to wonder this myself. How and *why* were we doing it? As if he could read my mind, he began to console me with one of my favorite Matthewisms. "Oh girl, you know what they say. You've gotta suffer if you wanna sing the blues." Yes, I nodded slowly, realizing that he was right. We *were* working in the trenches. We *had* been on the front line, as some of the first foreigners of a new wave of expats that weren't just here to surf. By doing business here, for better or for worse, we were collectively all helping to put Joyita on the map as a Panamanian tourist destination. And I *was* singing the blues because I was no longer learning though experience or divine gifts, but actually suffering. This was not the life I had imagined for myself. I needed something new, something different. Some magic. I didn't know how, but I knew I needed to reconnect to myself again.

We were still living in one of the hotel cabañas which we knew was a huge part of feeling trapped within our business. We were beginning to get more serious about wanting a proper house but still didn't have the capital or a building plan we could agree on. Skeech came by one day to explore the upper part of our property with Matt and see all the trails he and Fausti had been installing.

He and Matt were puttering around the yard and brainstorming when I came down from doing yoga up on top of the town water tank. I stopped and chattered with them, taking in the sunset. I was standing in a yogi squat on the trail above them chiming in occasionally. Skeech looked up at me as I began to move and stretch, twisting and clasping my hands behind my back still squatting down. "Why don't you guys build a yoga platform up here? Michelle is always practicing with friends and doesn't have a space to do it. Something basic, but to get you up here, away from the business and to start using this part of the property more."

Hmmm, now that got my attention! I certainly wasn't the strongest, or most flexible person in the world, but I loved yoga and in fact, I needed yoga in my life if I wanted to be pain-free. "You could build a little platform right there where she is, for three or four people, and then another down here where she could teach." Matt's wheels started spinning right away.

"Or, we build it on top of the *old* abandoned cement town water tank that's on our property and that way the yoga studio floor could become the roof for my workshop that I want to build somewhere. I could cut a door into the water tank and make that a tool shed/workspace." *Hmmm* I wondered how that was going to get us any closer to our goal of building a house for ourselves.

From Matt's perspective I *always* shot down his ideas, would drag my feet, and was slow to move forward on *everything*. For me, he was too quick to plow into something new without thinking things over, or before we could come to an agreement on design or materials. At times he would just build something the way he wanted when I wasn't there (something important like the restaurant bar) ignoring the features I wanted. This discussion began to travel down our familiar road, or what was beginning to feel like two very separate roads rather, as we tried to find common ground between our dramatically different perspectives once again.

"I like the idea, but if we go bigger and put a roof over it, that's no longer basic, and we would be spending money on something other than a house. Plus, I don't know if I would feel comfortable offering classes to the public if I am not an actual certified instructor."

"Yeah, but you teach your friends, and how many years of experience do you have?" Matt asked.

"About seven since I first taught my "Stretch Everything" class at the Kodiak Community College, but I don't know. I'd have to think about it."

"Where could you get certified?"

"Probably Costa Rica."

"How much is it?"

"I dunno, I'd have to look into it. They're usually one month 200-hour training programs that are pretty expensive, like $5,000. I'd want to think about how much that would actually enrich or change my practice and teaching style. Maybe I could *not* go, and just call myself a yoga *guide*."

"5,000 dollars! For one month!? And then you could teach those courses and charge that kind of money!?" Matt saw dollar signs once again as his sugar mama mentally made its way into the discussion.

"No, that's a longer training, like 500 or 1,000 hours. I'm not sure."

"Okay, well, maybe you could do that later. You could also use the space to do massages and so maybe it could be a wellness facility with other services and classes as well."

This was actually a really great idea! I was the only massage therapist living in Joyita and it would be nice to have a space to offer treatments to the public. *But* I noted to myself, all of this was more work, ***for me***. I pushed past the fact that this investment was not going to get us closer to living outside of our business and into this new possibility. And who knows, I thought, maybe my next border run to Costa Rica I could go check out some schools and travel on my own again. Travel and a yoga teacher training might be exactly the new thing or the magic I was in need of. It had been years since I had done any kind of training.

Matt was completely on board. I began to get my mojo back just researching the options. I had found a yoga studio in Montezuma that hosted regular training programs with visiting instructors. I also looked into the Nosara Yoga Institute that had an amazing reputation and where a good friend of mine had been certified. A loose plan was forming to visit these two places.

Since we had bought a car, I hadn't actually ridden the slow Joyita bus in years, and I wasn't looking forward to it. When my travel day came, I boarded and greeted familiar faces. I took a seat near a sweet elderly Señor, who along with his wife, I absolutely adored. They were both so loving, happy, and clear. "Michelita," he always called me, "where are you going?" And of course, he threw in the, "*sola*?" question because no one here could imagine I drove to Santiago by myself, much less travel to another country. "*Sí*," I rattled on about yoga and Matt staying to work. As we passed through the various neighboring villages other familiar faces began to board the bus, smile, and greet me by name. I was glowing with the joy of feeling recognized, of feeling like I belonged. I realized that even though I was leaving, some small part of me had arrived. Maybe I had not been fully accepted, but I was acknowledged and loved here.

When I got to Montezuma, it was easy to single out the attendees of the teacher training as there were about twenty women in spandex yoga pants milling about in this two road town. I spoke to a few women on the street explaining that I had traveled there to find out more about the program, to meet the instructor, and learn firsthand about their experience. "Well, you can probably find Melanie (the instructor) in the bar," one woman replied in an exasperated tone.

"In the bar?" I asked, taken aback. "Does she hang out there often?"

"She just started to. At lunch, *and* in the evening now that she's fucking a local guy that works there. It's really bullshit, you know. In the beginning of the program, she encouraged us all to take this time for ourselves and be mindful of where we put our energy and what we ingest in our bodies. She recommended we try to eat vegan while we are here and give up caffeine, and alcohol. And now there she is engaging in toxic behavior with this guy and drinking alcohol every single day."

This was about all I needed to hear to know Melanie was not going to be the yoga instructor for me, but I turned to the other two women for more. "Okay, but what do you think of the instruction itself?"

"I guess for the price, it's not that bad. I'm paying $2,400 to share a room with three other girls," one woman shared. "Most programs are about twice as much, but she told us to read five different books before we came and bring them, and she still hasn't gone over anything. We mostly just watch her and practice asana all day."

"I think that's all I need to hear, thank you."

"You'd be way better off paying more and receiving a higher quality education," the third woman chimed in.

The original whistle blower pointed to the beach front bar that sat at the end of the road and said, "I'm sure she's still there if you want to meet her." Why not, I thought. I had come all this way.

I walked to the open-air restaurant where there were a few people and a couple seated at rustic wooden tables, but only one fair skinned blonde woman, medium in stature, and seated alone at the bar. Knowing this was her from the photos on her website, I approached, greeted her by name and offered a handshake. This was met with an inquisitive look on her face which seemed to ask if finding her at a bar mid-day was suspect. I explained that I had traveled there from Panamá to learn more about her teacher training program. Melanie excused herself from her bar stool kissing her boyfriend goodbye and suggested we go talk on the beach. I took in the white sand beach and a palm tree that was nearly growing vertically behind Melanie as she began to swing herself around in dramatic arm sweeping movements.

She explained how the girls just didn't understand her and what she had with this guy. "They're all judging me, and think I'm being childish," she offered without me having mentioned a thing. She continued to move her arms around her head gracefully as if she was performing some sort of swimming ballet occasionally using the palm tree for balance. I thought how it would be impossible to make this shit up as I continued to listen and smile while she told me how much yoga experience she had in New York City and had suffered through a whole string of unhealthy relationships in the past. "This is different. I know this is different," she reassured me.

"Okay, well thank you," I said, ready to leave having learned nothing about the actual training itself.

"I'm sorry. I'm sorry if I shared too much. You can go to my website to read more about me, my experience, and the teacher trainings I lead."

"I have. Thanks. That's why I'm here."

"Okay, well maybe I'll see you again," she winced, realizing how bad of an impression she had just made. "My next program is in December." *If* there is a next program, I thought as I walked away. I did go look at the studio and the rooms in the event that another teacher was to offer a training there any time soon, but the real magic of this journey really began for me after I headed northwest to the beach town of Nosara to check out the Yoga Institute.

One of the first people I met there while I still had my backpack on and was unsure of where I was going to stay was an American girl named Carlie. She was a recent graduate of the Nosara Yoga Institute and had nothing but good things to say about it. She was also housesitting for an American who had a large home and a pool. After chatting for a while, she said she would call him and see if I could stay in his open-air loft above the outdoor kitchen overlooking the pool. With that done, I went with my new friend to get settled into my free temporary home. She and I spent the evening together cooking, talking, and laughing. Even after the owner and his friend came back from San José, I continued to stay there and hang out with them as they were super relaxed.

Because of the institute, Nosara is a yoga town. A surf and yoga town. I had never seen anything like it. Even though there wasn't a teacher training or any public classes taking place at the institute, there were still people everywhere with yoga mats in hand, their dogs and surf boards at their sides. The school bookstore was open, and I met Jasmine, the program director who was super helpful and gave me a professional folder with lots of information about the training. Carlie had mentioned that the school offered partial scholarships at that time, so I asked Jasmine about it. She told me to write to her if I was serious about attending and she would send me a scholarship form to fill out to apply. This ten-day adventure filled my soul, and I returned home excited to talk to Matt about attending the Yoga Institute's fall program.

"$3,800 is a lot of money, especially during the low season when we have no income, and I don't really want to put it on a credit card."

I agreed but thought that going to look at schools meant he was fully on board with this. *He* was the one so hot to build the yoga studio and saying I was always putting the breaks on everything. He already had the metal structure built, wood flooring ordered, and had asked me to draw out giant yoga poses to bend and weld to form the guardrail. "I'm just going to write them and apply for a half scholarship to see if I can get it," I said feeling disappointed by his sudden change of heart.

"All right, but $1,900 is still a lot right now, and that doesn't include food or housing. We will still have to pay for that. I'm not saying to not go *ever*; I just think maybe we should wait until high season begins and we have more income."

"The studio will be finished, and I want to be able to offer yoga this next high season." Exhausted by his realism and knowing that his bark was worse than his bite I threw in, "Well, maybe there will be some sort of miracle. The money could come from somewhere completely unexpected. I'm just going to apply," which actually gave me an idea.

When the yoga institute accepted my application for a half scholarship I decided to talk to my parents before I said anything to Matt. I hadn't asked them for help since they paid for my education at the Florida School of Massage ten years ago, and that had been with money they had saved for my college education. This was education too, and I didn't know if there was anything left, but I thought to ask. I spoke to my mom and told her about the institute, the program, and our plan to open the first yoga studio in Joyita. And then I finally popped the question. "No," she responded, meaning I had no more college education money, "but just the other day I was going through some old paperwork we have for you and found some savings bonds that Granny had given you when you were baby that still haven't been cashed. Let me see how much there is, and I'll let you know."

When she sent me an email later that day to tell me there was $1,900, I was over the moon! That was the exact cost of the program after the scholarship! It was absolutely meant to be! It was a sign! The first one I had received in what felt like a very long time!

Chapter 20

Waking Up.... Again

When it came time to leave for my yoga teacher training, there was *nothing* going on in Playa Joyita. It was early November, and we were deep into the low season and one of the rainiest months of the year. I had decided not to book my housing through the school even though that was what they recommended. Instead, I was trying to find my way back to my default operating system of leaving "all doors open" for any and all (especially cheaper) opportunities to present themselves. I was hoping to arrive two days before the course started to get my feet on the ground and to begin house hunting, but when I got to the rough border town in the pouring down rain and was looking to board a north bound bus, I was told *no hay paso* or there is no passing. The road was closed due to flooding. "*¿Hace cuánto tiempo?*" I asked, wondering how long it had been closed and how long they suspected it would take to drain, essentially becoming that annoying tourist who asks the ridiculous question of when it's supposed to stop raining. "*Nadie se sabe*," I was told, which of course, no one knows, and the rain was still coming down in full force filling the dingy streets of Paso Canoas (Canoe Passing) with rapidly moving streams of dirty brown water.

I brainstormed my options. I could sit in a hotel in this border town possibly for *days* until the weather and road conditions improve. I could contact the school and see if they still planned on starting the program on time, go the six hours back home and try again in a few days, or *fly*. I knew there was a small airport in the port town of Golfito where we had looked at property once upon a time and had visited on various occasions since. Golfito was only a thirty-minute bus ride from the border, and I imagined that road was still passable, so I headed to the airport by bus and then taxi. After speaking to the male receptionist, I learned that the cloud ceiling and visibility was too low for the small national airlines to legally fly, but that if I wanted, I could add my name to a list of people who were willing to take a charter flight at their own risk, whenever the sky lifted enough to (fingers crossed) safely fly. "How much will that be?" I asked.

"It depends how many people there are to share the cost. Right now, there are 1, 2, 3, … seven people waiting. You are the eighth. If they send a twelve-seater it will be about $120 each right now with eight people."

"Okay, I'd like to add my name to the list please," I said, hoping I could at least get to San José that night. I was told to take a seat and wait with the other passengers, some of whom I soon learned had already been waiting there for two days. I noted that in the fifteen years that I hadn't watched the news, this was the first time it had actually affected me, having no idea that there was a storm warning in Costa Rica. I made small talk with this new cast of characters who were now on my same adventure, looked at the nearby lush hillside to gauge the cloud height against the backdrop of the jungle, and wrote in my journal. When we were losing daylight, the receptionist told us he would be closing in thirty minutes and asked if we wanted him to call in a hotel reservation and transportation to leave for the day. "You can come back first thing in the morning. With a little bit of luck, the sky will have lifted by then." We all agreed, told him how many rooms we needed, and headed over to the Golfito Marina Hotel in a couple of taxis. I had dinner and watched the news with the two Mexican businessmen and a Peruvian who I had met at the airport. I became lost in their rapid chatter, so I turned my attention to the television as Costa Rica declared they were in a state of natural disaster. The news coverage showed collapsed bridges, chocolatey rivers overflowing, and the damage from avalanches which continued.

Over breakfast, the hotel receptionist let us know that a plane would be arriving for us at ten a.m., but we needed to head to the airport first thing to confirm and pay for our reservation. The sky had lifted, and the flight in this tiny charter plane was amazing! We were all given a headset and could hear and see as the pilot pointed out what we may never see again; the many valleys that were still flooded and the carless roads that looked like brown rivers winding around the hillsides not far below.

I had checked in with the school the night before to see if the road was passable to Nosara and if the course was still going to start on time. I was told the program was still a go, but I would need to *fly* from the smaller International Airport Tobias Bolanos in San José. When we landed, I checked with the pilot to see what airport we were at and told him where I needed to be. "That's a $30 taxi ride to get to the other side of the city," he told me. "I have another flight departing from there and need to move the aircraft. I can take you with me, for free." *Weeeeeeiiiiii!* I was elated! This free plane ride was an unimaginable best case scenario times 100 and told me I was exactly where I needed to be. I sent up my gratitude. *Thank you! Thank You! Thank You Universe!*

Even after walking along the runway to the other hanger and waiting for clearance, I arrived at Tobias Bolanos airport in less time than it would have taken in a taxi and profusely thanked the pilot. I would have to pay for two more unexpected flights, so this was a serious silver lining, literally, in the lifting clouds. I walked in to book my flight and made my way to the gate where I was immediately able to identify and gravitate towards other yogis headed to Nosara. All three had made the mistake of going to the wrong airport and paid $30 *twice* in taxis. As two continued to carry on, bitch and complain, I gently shared my good fortune. The other, a young woman from San Francisco, began to play her banjo and sing, drowning out their negativity. I sang along to the songs I knew, and she and I made a nice connection.

Once in Liberia, we picked up more displaced yogis and took another small plane to Nosara, eventually finding ourselves in the bookstore which was buzzing with everyone checking in and getting pointed in the right direction towards their housing. When Jasmine (the director I had met on my trip before) got to me, she seemed confused. "I don't have you down for any housing," she said.

"Yeah, I'm going to look at a few places now."

"Why and where?" she asked, looking at me puzzled. After I described the few options I had seen online she told me, "Those are really far away. Everything we recommend is within walking distance of the school so you can come and go safely between short breaks."

"Well," I asked reluctantly, but with the awareness that the program was going to start the next morning, "Do you still have anything available through the school?"

"I have a shared with one other person for $350. It doesn't have a proper kitchen. It has a hot plate and a small fridge, so you have to use the bathroom sink for cooking and to do dishes. It's with Layla."

The price was right, but "Who's Layla?" I asked. Because aside from saving, I was hoping to have my own place to get a break from the group therapy dynamic that I imagined would be a huge part of the program.

"The girl with the guitar that you came in with."

Ahhhhh, a light went on. My new favorite friend! I had forgotten her name. That's perfect, I thought, and could be the whole reason I had held off on housing all along.

"Ummm, okay, let me check with her," I said. After speaking with Layla and her being completely open, knowing that she signed up to share with someone, I agreed, happy to have a laid-back California-girl musician for a roommate.

After 6:30 a.m. yoga the following morning, the first thing they talked about in the program was "sacred space" which has become a buzzword today, but this was the first time I had ever heard these two words together. They explained that sacred space is about each of us agreeing to provide a safe container wherein we could all feel free to express ourselves without judgment, as well as the importance of honoring the fact that everyone is experiencing the program in their own way. They also said it was possible that some of the content would feel deeply relevant to us, and at other times, it would not make sense or be inviting. They assumed we were all there to deepen our self-awareness and reminded us that each individual experience was equally valid. They discouraged gossip and urged us to not speak about how we perceived anyone else's experience or behavior in the group, neither bad nor good. "It is imperative that you all feel safe and supported to speak and experience your own personal truth without the fear of being judged or criticized." This turned a light on for me as I realized what a rarity this was in the world.

They asked us to write down our intention for coming to the training. Sensing that what I was about to experience was going to be far greater than anything I had imagined, I wrote, "My *original* intention was to deepen my own yoga practice and work on my alignment so that I can guide more confidently." Shortly after I wrote that, we were told that the Yoga Institute did not focus on alignment and therefore had no mirrors in the studio. They taught with more emphasis on how the pose *feels* within your body because they understood that we are all very different anatomically. I found this slightly annoying because I wasn't very flexible and wanted to be sure I "looked right" when I was teaching in front of a group of people, but that idea quickly began to fade as I let go of my idea of yoga being a physical practice and started to melt back into spirituality, something I realized had been lost to me for some time now.

As we were presented with yoga philosophy, it seemed to not make sense for the majority, but it was definitely reawakening something within me. When they spoke about Samadhi or those momentary feelings of enlightenment that come to us, I felt a familiar tingling sensation in my body, a remembrance of merging with the one or becoming part of something greater than myself. A few days later, when they mentioned that yoga was a method for achieving an altered state of consciousness naturally without the use of drugs, my heart began to beat faster, knowing that these were teachings that had never been explained to me throughout all of my drug use. I realized that I hadn't done psychedelics in over seven years since my NDE, and I hadn't even given any real thought to those experiences in just about that long! I had become so consumed with being a wife, a stepmom, and especially a business owner, that I had brushed a lot of my esoterisms under the rug. So much so, that I had forgotten yoga was a spiritual practice at all! For *years* now I had been practicing yoga and guiding friends through what I thought of as "just stretching" to help relieve chronic pain and for relaxation. Now I asked myself if I had fallen so deep into the reality trap that I had given up on or forgotten not only that yoga was a spiritual practice, but about the spiritual aspect of my journey here on Earth. It made me sad to think that even *I* had begun to refer to the more spiritual period of my life as my "teenage rebellion." Once upon a time, I knew it wasn't that. I was *not* lost. I was trying to remain *found*; to stay connected to Source and Universal truth; and not become diluted by the pressures of society and our collective "reality."

Before coming to Nosara, I hadn't really considered there would be any spiritual depth to this program, but I was realizing this was exactly what I needed. I was no longer here to work on my *physical* alignment, but to align with the Divine once again, and to realign with myself, my goals, and my true nature. Having been of service to so many others over the last few years, I had totally forgotten about who I was, the importance of self-love, and staying connected to Source and the fountain of unconditional love. I saw why I had been drawn here to this "self-inquiry of yoga" (as they called the program) which they said was an invitation to come home to our own inner wisdom, our own bodies, and our own truth. Fireworks went off not only in my mind, but my heart as well!

All of this had me back in that high, psychedelic, blissful state *naturally*. Layla, our neighbor Jessica, and I were an ecstatic trio loving every minute of the training and our time together cooking, laughing, studying, and singing. Because the school used a silly OM song to teach the Sanskrit names for each posture (Tadasana OM, Tadasana OM, Tadasana OM), OMing was at the forefront of our minds. The three of us would walk the jungle trail home for breaks and make up our own OM songs. "OM, OM on the Range," and "Take me OM, country road, to the place, I belong, IN SHAVASANA." We laughed uncontrollably at our own brilliance and ridiculousness. When we'd get home, Layla would attempt to play the full version on her banjo or mandolin which was perfect for country OM songs. The two of us spent the little time we had outside of the program drawing silly yoga comic strips and singing our favorite songs: Cat Stevens, "If You Want to Sing Out, Sing Out" and The Bare Necessities (from the Jungle Book movie) which for me, perfectly embodied our jungle experience and echoed my earlier life philosophy. "Forget about your worries and your strife, I mean the bare necessities, Old Mother Nature's recipes, that brings the bare necessities of life."[24] We were so happy within ourselves and with the yoga practice and teachings. We were living effortlessly within and respecting the sacred space that had been established at the beginning of the program, never once speaking about anyone else in the group.

As I continued to expand, Matt was hearing nothing from me. I called him once via Skype at the Internet Café to let him know I had arrived safely, but the call dropped. Without a smartphone, wifi or even a regular phone in our room, I was only communicating with him via email every so often. And even still, sitting in an Internet Café was *not* how I wanted to be spending my short breaks away from class, from the pressures of everyday life, and from La Buena Vida. I perceived this moment as a crossroads in my life. Having realized just how different Matt and I were, and how intense the life we had created had become, I knew things couldn't continue like this, *not for me*. Though he *had* quit drinking, it had only been about six months, and I was still waiting for the other shoe to drop and wondered where that would lead me. He

---

[24] Lyrics from the song The Bare Necessities written by Terry Gilkyson which was featured in the 1967 Disney animated film The Jungle Book

had traded alcohol for drinking sodas and working with the same intensity that he had put into drinking at the height of his alcoholism. His values were so completely different from mine that I knew something had to shift, but I didn't know *who* or *what* needed to change. I wanted to take advantage of this opportunity and enjoy every moment of focusing on me and my growth. I was singing, journaling, cooking good food with Layla, and doing more than nine hours of yoga and study per day. But Matt was becoming completely unraveled.

As I continued reconnecting to me, to my path, and to my purpose, Matt's email messages were becoming more and more desperate. He told me he was going crazy without me, and how much he missed me and wanted to hear my voice. In the past, we would go weeks without talking. While he was out fishing or one of us was away from Joyita we had no way to communicate with one another and neither of us had ever had an issue with it. But now, for the first time in the seven years we had been together, he seemed highly insecure. Maybe he too sensed this was a pivotal moment for me. Maybe he had thought the change I needed might be us separating. Or perhaps he was misinterpreting my renewed interest in myself as interest in someone else. Maybe he was afraid I would meet someone "more like-minded" here who was spiritual and *did* share my same values. Whatever it was, it was obvious he was really struggling without me, so I finally attempted to call him for the first time in three weeks. I wished him a Happy Thanksgiving and told him about the program and how much I was loving it. He told me that he was doing a radical cleanse and had quit drinking caffeine and eating sugar. He was reading one of my books, "Healing with Whole Foods" by Paul

Pitchford and was going through his own self-transformation, further detoxifying his system. This was not something he had ever done before. *This was change,* I thought, both surprised and impressed by his initiative to work on himself as well. As I communicated that I was proud of him, I wondered if this meant he too was working on his flexibility and would be willing to shift his perspectives when it came to his values and the commitment that I thought we had both made to go into business with one another. He was very grateful for my call, thanking me profusely. Before we ended our conversation, I said I'd try to call one more time before I left Nosara.

As the program was winding down, a few scandals blew up with our neighbor Jessica right smack dab in the middle of one of them. Layla and I had been so sing-songy happy in our own world, we were completely surprised by all of it. A number of students voiced that they were upset by the lack of "vetting" that was conducted when accepting people into the program. They were complaining about the students who had only done yoga once prior to this training or who were there and knew nothing about yoga and therefore did not share their yoga mindset, specifically an American ex-cop that had been injured on the job, and the two other American men who had gravitated together into their trio of new friends. The argument was that the owners cared more about quantity and their earning potential, and not quality, having allowed less experienced or "unqualified" yogis to join the training. There were comments about these three not taking the program seriously, arriving late, or sometimes not at all. I was shocked! I had barely noticed anyone else's attendance, and certainly didn't find myself being distracted by it! This seemed to go completely against the idea of non-judgment and understanding that we were all on a different journey, or even aside from sacred space, what about the preschool lesson of "Don't worry about what anyone else is doing, just worry about yourself?" A counter argument to holding non-judgmental sacred space was made that these three were not dedicating themselves to self-discovery *at all* and therefore some were struggling with honoring their disruptive behavior.

Then there was the Jessica scandal. Accusations were being made that one of the (other) male students had been touching or adjusting her "inappropriately." Apparently, this had already been brought to the owners' attention and they had immediately addressed it. Jessica had responded that no, that was not the case. The two of them were friends, and she both trusted and felt safe in his presence. And in fact, I knew that the two of them had shared a few nights out together, so my thought was maybe it was consensual inappropriate touch that Jessica did not want him to get in trouble for. All of this came out as the shit hit the fan during class one morning and we lost a complete half day of instruction to emotional back and forth discussions and someone failing to own up to a hurtful anonymous email that the owners had received and read out loud.

Layla and I left the shala that morning completely flabbergasted and with all of the wind taken out of our OM singing sails. We walked the trail in silence for the first time since the program had begun. It was hard to believe that people were having such a different experience, and I wondered how we can personally grow or focus on love if our energy is spent on judging, criticizing, or complaining about others, or even ourselves. We had done such a great job just focusing on ourselves and being playful, especially Jessica, who hadn't shared any of this with us at all. A light went on! At home I had been taking myself far too seriously. I hadn't been "just worrying about myself" either! Instead of living in gratitude, singing, dancing and celebrating everything we had created, I had been complaining, criticizing, and focusing on it being too much or on Matt not being enough! My attention was no longer flowing into the magic of gratitude and the wonder of what could be. I was stuck in "what is" or "what is not." I wondered if I would be able to maintain my focus and this sense of joy and playfulness when I got back to Joyita. Because as I well knew, we were not on vacation, and we were certainly not living in the sacred space of a yoga retreat setting. This had been a great reset, but I wasn't sure if it was really sustainable once I got home and knew I would be inundated with work, Matt's yang, and the complexities of small village life again.

As the program wrapped up, I realized that yoga is so much more than stretching and holding postures. Yoga is *listening* to the self. It's observing your body, your *mind*, and *your actions* in a state of non-judgment. It's observing how we move through life, our interactions, and our behavior patterns. Yoga is being kind to ourselves and making the necessary adjustments as we go along. Not adjusting solely our posture, but having flexibility with our perspectives, our attitudes, habits, and behavior so that we can continue to grow into a fuller and more honest version of ourselves. The program had brought me back to some of the same realizations I had through my travels and the use of psychedelics; that we are not our physical bodies. As the famous quote goes, "We are not human beings having a spiritual experience, we are spiritual beings having a human experience."[25] I knew I had a lot of work to do when I got home if I wanted to try to bring back this new found sense of self, non-judgment, and spirituality to my everyday life, as well as salvage the "good life" we had created. I also knew breathwork and yoga alone were not going to do it and hoped Matt was willing to make some necessary adjustments as well.

---

[25] Though no source is cited, this quote is often credited to the French philosopher Pierre Teilhard de Chardin

Chapter 21

Integration?

I was excited to get home to the new treetop yoga studio and share more details about the program with Matt, but upon my return he had no time for me. He was busy entertaining some older Americans who were looking to invest in the Joyita area. There I was, day one back at home, and already feeling dejected by our contrasting values. Matt had been so desperate to talk to me on the phone while I was gone, and now that I was home, I had to tag along with him and these "investors" if I wanted to have any time together at all. While he was off running around, sharing his local knowledge and showing them property, he was showing me that nothing on his part had really changed. After this group of guys left, we were able to go back to our same old conversation about him overworking and me feeling overworked. I would have loved to share more time and responsibilities at La Buena Vida with him, but I could see his financial drive was probably not going to change. We discussed *his* solution for me to delegate more and hire a manager. We agreed that I should move forward and actively look for someone by running an online ad.

The first young woman I hired was a gem! She was a Peruvian American who loved traveling, diving, and spoke fluent Spanish. For her, working in a place like Joyita allowed her to form relationships with our local employees and gain an even deeper understanding of Panamanian culture. She and I developed a unique relationship, and she returned many times. Ten years her senior, I became her mother-sister-boss-friend as Debra had been mine. A succession of managers came and went after her: an amazing Canadian couple, a girlfriend from Alaska, our niece who we were thrilled to have close by, and eventually a Panamanian yoga instructor. This did give both of us more time and freedom for other things in our lives. I was creating more art, able to go to the beach more often, give massages, and teach yoga classes. Matt started a construction company and got more into surfing, enjoying great waves at The Point.

We could only afford to pay someone in the high season and occasionally would splurge in the mid-season or look for hotel sitters so we could go travel when things were slow. But ultimately, orchestrating La Buena Vida was my job and everything would fall on me once again between managers, to train managers, and give them direction. By the time someone new arrived, I would be in need of some serious support, but hiring could be completely hit or miss. I would share every detail about the job and Joyita. I would explain how far it was from a regular grocery store; the weather; the bugs; that they would be working with Spanish speaking staff; and the new hire was coming to support *us*, but there was no way to predict if people would be able to adapt. Periodically, a manager would arrive who really struggled with how basic life was in Joyita, the heat, the bugs, or the remoteness. You name it, many were out of their comfort zone with it, and *they* would be in need of more support than I could realistically give them. This caused me to become even more spent, and on the verge of my first nervous breakdown.

We were still living onsite in our first cabaña with three other rentals. Aside from short breaks (if I went on a walk or to the beach) I could never get away from work or guests. Manager or no manager, from the moment I stepped out of our front door, I may have to greet guests, answer their questions, or start problem solving. Sometimes they even knocked on our door with questions. Once we had people just walk into our home without knocking, mistaking it for the reception! We were still discussing the construction of our house and had even applied for a construction loan (twice) but interest rates were really high. Instead, we had decided to convert Matt's shop under the yoga studio into a small living space for ourselves. This was an even smaller space than where we were living (300 square feet), but it sat in the treetops and put a little more distance between us and the business. Matt set to work converting the old cement town water tank into a room for Gabe which would give us all a little more privacy. He created a yoga themed bathroom with the sink in bridge pose that we would share with yoga students. We called our new dwelling "the bird cage" because Matt put metal screening along the upper half of two of our bedroom walls. It felt as if we were living amongst the birds, in a cage, in the treetops. Waking up with the sunrise and watching nature unfold while lying in bed every morning was definitely a game changer. I began starting my days in the yoga studio that was right overhead. We didn't have a kitchen, so we were still eating all of our meals in the restaurant, usually turning off the lights at night and sitting in the dark so no one would bother us. We had a coffee maker which was key. I would try to be sufficiently meditated and caffeinated before I went down the hill so I'd be prepared for anything that may come my way. And come my way it did because after finally having access to medium speed Internet (in 2011), we were beginning to feel the effects of the rapidly changing tourism industry.

Slowly but surely, nearly all of the twenty-some hotels that now existed in Joyita were listed on Booking. Matt was pressuring me to do the same, saying we were losing lots of business without it, but I had just finally integrated an online calendar where guests could book directly. It was a big step for me that came with some real consequences. In the past, if people wanted to reserve a room, they would have to email to ask about availability and a number of other questions. An automatic booking system made it less hands on for me (and our managers), which was a good thing, but we had to have reliable Internet and remember to check and update both our paper calendar and the online calendar constantly. For the first time ever, no prior correspondence with future guests looking to make a reservation was necessary. This meant we were spending less time answering people's general questions, but it was apparent that they were spending less time on our website or reading about Joyita in general. Gone were the days of travel agent brochures and reading an entire book about the country you would soon be visiting. Now, with just a click of a button, a trip was planned. If this was done on one of the mega-search engine sites, there seemed to be an even bigger disconnect as to where they were actually going. The banner on some of these booking agent websites might show a city skyline or a beautiful coastline in Mexico, offering round trip flight deals to New York City or Cancun. After glimpsing a few photos of hotels with pools (the three that existed in Joyita at that time) while scrolling the hospitality options, future visitors could easily hold all of these images of paradise or luxury in their minds when thinking of their future stay. If they were to look at an online map of the village when choosing their hotel, they would see it sprinkled with many tourist businesses, but they would not see the modest local homes or the large empty cow fields that were located in between these places. Nope, with the same click of a button people had used to make their European holiday reservations and to book their Panama City skyscraper hotel, they were able to book a one-star hotel in Joyita. So of course they would have similar expectations for their upcoming stay. *And* these huge Dutch (Booking) and American owned corporations (like Expedia) were earning 15% of all the hospitality income from a tiny rural Panamanian village.

Then there were the reviews that I began pulling my hair out over. I hated TripDispiser and the fact that we did not personally list our business, nor did we have any choice about it being listed there. In my mind they were extortionists, forcing businesses to pay (at that time roughly $800 per year) in order to add or change photos and for a link to their website. With this being the world's most frequently visited travel site, as a small business, we had no choice but to pay more than our monthly car insurance payment (again, to a large *multi-billion-dollar* American corporation) so that the hotel would not lose visibility or click-ability. In fact, without our business on these booking platforms, it was getting harder and harder for anyone to find our website. The adventure traveler was dying, along with my *ganas* (desire) to spend much time with the guests, and I certainly didn't want to spend my days on the computer checking for reservations, updating the online calendar, creating competitive pricing promotions, and replying to reviews. But if we wanted to compete with our friends and neighbors, the pressure from these mega-corporations was definitely there to do so.

Something a past guest had told me rang in my ears. He said that while he was traveling, a Mexican señora once told him, "Bad roads bring good people, but good roads bring all sorts of people." Throw in the Internet, I thought, and it brings all sorts of expectations. Add consumer reviews to the mix, and now we had non-guests leaving one-star reviews simply because they didn't like our restaurant hours or wifi policy. Too much authority and power had been placed in the hands of travelers who hadn't taken the time to look into where they were going and to think about what that actually means. All the business owners in Joyita were doing their best to try to provide visitors with an amazing experience, but it was very difficult with the limited resources we actually had available to us.

The wifi password was now the first thing people asked for when they checked in. Not to see the room, to ask how far of a walk it was to the beach, or go to check out the village. Nope, they needed to get online. People had no idea where they were so they would attempt to use the slow Internet to book a local tour, not knowing it was just a three-minute walk down the road to talk directly to the tour operator. Some refused to listen to my verbal directions or to take a paper map, insisting they needed to download navigation when I knew it wouldn't work on the roads they were going to take. Things were beginning to slow down and become surreal for me once again, but not in a psychedelic-spiritual-life-is-a-movie sort of way that I had experienced before. More in an underwater-I-can't-breathe-I-am-becoming-so-overwhelmed kind of drowning sensation.

Two years had passed since my yoga training and I was still practicing almost daily as an effort to cultivate more inner peace which would hopefully overflow onto guests. But it was becoming increasingly more difficult for me to sympathize with people who became unraveled without their modern-day conveniences (mainly the speed of the Internet and the regular power outages) while on vacation for just a few days. During some of my lower moments I would say things like, "Yes, and imagine, *we* are trying to run a business here *year-round*," which normally did not land well. I had one young European woman come to me to report that their safe was not working in the room. "Yes, I know. It hasn't been working for months," I explained, probably a little too honestly, but the batteries had run out and all the guests had walked off with the keys. Matt had known and still hadn't done anything about it, so as I saw it, it was completely out of my hands.

"Well, online it said the room came with a safe. We booked this room for the safe," she said, clearly wanting me to remedy the situation.

"You booked the room *for the safe!?* Not the beautiful tile work, the air conditioning, the location, the amazing outdoor shower?" I asked sarcastically, and assumed a demand for a discount was on the horizon.

"Yes, we were planning on putting our money and passports in the safe, so I'd like to know just what you suggest that we do?"

"Uhhhhh," I let out an annoyed sigh, but she had asked, and I finally saw a way to implement a spiritual lesson into one of my discords. So my response was, "I dunno, *Trust*?"

Clearly this woman was not ready for this teaching, as she became unraveled, and the whole thing ended with a free upgrade to a nicer room with a working safe.

"Maybe we should rent the hotel." Matt suggested during one of my rants, but neither one of us wanted to risk the business's reputation being ruined or having it returned in ruins.

"Let's buy Dante's house," he pressed yet again. Matt had been trying to talk me into buying another house off-site that also had an ocean view of the surf point, which made it extra appealing to him. Dante was a friend, and he was willing to finance us interest free. This was tempting, but a five-year loan would leave us with some steep payments. The house was small, but it was already built, and we could actually drive to it. The house we were talking about building on our hillside would never have car access, only a footpath. But I felt as if we were just arriving at the doorstep to more financial freedom, where once through, we would have enough income to travel more and begin to save for Gabe's college education if he chose to go in five years.

I knew I needed something to change but wasn't 100% sure this was it. As Matt continued to try to push me forward, I reverted to contemplation which was always perceived as slowing us down. "We don't have to move there right away. We can rent it out in the beginning, and it will pay for itself." This was his repeated argument, but it just wasn't true for me. For one, even if we did rent it twelve months a year at $600 per month, it would *not* pay for itself. Also, it was unrealistic that we could rent it out year-round in such a seasonal economy. He was *all*, and I was *or nothing*, and we were immobile once again.

After each of the missteps I had with guests or a circular conversation with Matt, I was trying to apply my yoga and look at it from a place of non-judgment so as to learn from every interaction. I knew buying Dante's house would be *more* in the sense that it was another financial responsibility, but I also knew it was an asset. Matt was trying to improve our, *especially my*, quality of life by moving us away from our business. I began to apply the self-inquiry of yoga and the inner-wisdom of every three-year-old to my life by asking myself why, and why, and why. Why was I resistant to Matt's perpetual business ideas and his desire for us to "succeed?" Why don't I want this cute little ocean view house our friend is willing to finance for us especially after having lived *really* minimally for so many years? Why am I afraid of having too much? Afraid of *looking* successful?

I realized that my entire adult life I had been "resisting against the system," pushing back against a society that places so much value on money and hard work.[26] And being surrounded by so many have-nots, it was difficult to allow myself to have more. I felt guilty that I was charging $60 *an hour* for a massage, when a *day's* wage for hard physical labor working in the heat with a shovel or

[26] Bob Marley & The Wailers, "One Drop," track #7 on *Survival*, Island Records/Tough Gong, 1979, vinyl

machete was $20 or $25. Buying this house and moving "on top of the hill" symbolized that I had made it to the top, and for me, that meant someone was on the bottom. I wasn't sure that was the place I wanted to be. My beliefs around money were a tangled up sticky mess of hippie ideology in a capitalistic world, living amongst poverty and scarcity mentality. If I was being completely honest with myself, I knew I was competitive by nature, and that I *did* want to succeed. But there was guilt and shame wrapped up around that, and I certainly didn't want to be *perceived* as being successful. I knew that I couldn't say yes to every one of Matt's business ideas, or he'd be off setting up some sort of distribution warehouse in China. At the same time, I also needed to work on my view of money and success for us to move forward together.

Chapter 22

Be Careful What You Wish For

I finally agreed to buy the house, and Matt agreed to oversee renting it out. "Oceanview Cottage" on Airbnb wasn't a stretch, but just as I had imagined, getting more than $600 a month for it was. It was about 600 square feet with a floorplan that was not focused on the view of the surf point, but instead, the kitchen looked out across the top of the palm trees at the Estero Beach in the distance. Aside from about four different styles of shiny brown tiles, the furniture was basic, but we couldn't afford to do more with it. The windows were jalousie style with glass slats that you crank open or closed and were covered with metal bars, so the beautiful ocean view was covered with these ugly windows and rusty metal security bars. Still, it had potential, and it was looking like we would eventually move here one day and not to our disputed dream home above the hotel.

We were taking the necessary steps to get ourselves further away from our business. We envisioned the bird cage becoming manager housing someday. Our business was too small to pay for or need 24-

hour reception, but due to late check ins, lost keys, snakes in the rooms, as a general presence for security's sake, or any other emergency, we did need to have someone onsite. We had extended the yoga studio and added another apartment underneath the addition to house seasonal yoga instructors and massage therapists. This was to expand our wellness program by offering more classes, retreats, and workshops because ultimately, teaching yoga and giving multiple massages daily, in addition to overseeing the restaurant and hotel operations, was just not sustainable. Now, depending on our live-in instructors, we were offering dance classes as well as yoga to the kids in the village for free. We also hosted Pilates, Thai Yoga Massage, moon ceremonies, ecstatic dance, yoga retreats, and any other creative endeavor we came up with. I was in my late thirties and was probably in the best physical shape of my life. On a really good day, I felt as if I was at the top of my game. I had carved out a wellness niche for our business which was something I was passionate about that no one else was offering. Though the community art workshop had faded, I was continuing to manage the recycle center and volunteer at the local school. On a bad day, I felt as if "no one" was helping me with *community* projects, and that it was all way too much, and not at all the simple life I had imagined for myself. I realized I had two choices; to either continue to work on my internal environment and adjust my perception of the external or make lasting changes that would affect the world around me. I decided that the volunteering had to give, at least temporarily. I had started these endeavors because they were important to me, but I had been continuing out of obligation for some time, and with resentment towards others who I viewed as "not doing their part." I realized I was falling into a negative space worrying about what other people *weren't* doing to help me, which was clouding something that I had started to make a positive change with unfounded judgment and criticism.

I knew that another aspect of my internal environment was that I cared too much about my external circumstances; La Buena Vida and other peoples' opinions of it, or me. La Buena Vida was my baby, and at times I took it personally if guests were critical or failed to realize everything that had gone into the building of what we were now calling our "artistic hotel." We put so much effort into providing things like feta cheese and sun-dried tomatoes which came from six hours away in Panama City so that guests could enjoy a Greek salad or Mediterranean wrap. Part of my problem was perfectionism. I wanted everything to be perfect, but I knew in my heart of hearts that perfect is subjective. So no matter what we did or how hard we worked, we were never going to meet everyone's expectations. Plus, maintenance in the tropics is a bitch and our financial resources (plus Matt's willingness and availability) were limited. Certified plumbers, electricians, A/C technicians, repairmen, and so on were two hours away and $100 minimum to make the trip to Joyita. Before making an unnecessary call, we would look to Matt to solve these bigger issues first. When we would call him to describe the latest problem, he would become annoyed, usually putting me or our managers off on someone else.

"Did you tell Fausti?" was normally his first response.

"Yes, but he wasn't sure what the problem was, and I really don't want him messing with the electricity."

"Call Bobo," he would say routinely, who was his right-hand man in his construction company, but I didn't want to call Bobo and work closely with him. I wanted to work together and have the support of my husband. That's why we opened this business together. "That's a waste of my time," would be his final response which gave me no other option than to bother Bobo afterhours and hope he would come.

When Matt told me he had an opportunity to open another hotel with a friend and his business partner in his construction company, I was floored. I couldn't believe that our hotel was a waste of his time and we had a whole list of unfinished projects and work that needed to be done, but he was thinking about opening another!?

"Absolutely not," was my response, not able to imagine how he could spend even less time within La Buena Vida. "We created this business together, and *you're the one* who wanted to offer high end rooms, to-go lunches, laundry service for the public, etcetera, and then you just left me here alone to manage all your great ideas!"

"This will be different. For one, they are going to be mini-apartments which there is a real need for in this town. *And*, it's going to run itself. Michelle, we poured our hearts and souls into La Buena Vida, and that's part of the problem. You take everything so personally and want to give such customized attention. This is going to be like the Holiday Inn. No hand holding or even showing them to their room. We're going to build it like a standard hotel and have managers that will be like, 'here's your key, room one. Enjoy your stay, bye bye'."

Errrrr, I couldn't believe what I was hearing! I knew people would have the same expectations everywhere and I immediately began to put the brakes on. Aside from our hotel, Matt was now managing at least ten other rentals that constantly needed work or had problems. His tenants would come to La Buena Vida to pay their rent or complain because he wasn't responding to their phone calls. Out of self-perseverance, I decided I could *not* take this on as well and this is where I began to draw a line. These were his responsibilities and what *he* had committed to thinking it was *so easy*. I told his tenants I had nothing to do with their rental property and they would have to speak with Matt directly. In my mind, he clearly had too much on his plate. If he couldn't keep up with his existing responsibilities, how was he going to take on more? Bob Marley's words continued to play in my head, "Now you get what you want, do you want more? You think it's the end, but it's just the beginning…"[27]

"You need to think outside of the box. I'm trying to create more opportunities and wealth for us."

"*Yah, well*, because you don't have the time or energy to maintain what you've got going on inside the box, *I've* been the one on the front line taking all the heat for your neglect."

"Let's sell then," was his solution.

"Sell our dream, so you can go off and build the same dream somewhere else with someone else!? We agreed to do this together, so I don't think it's fair if I have to give up my dream because you're no longer willing to help me."

"Michelle, it's not that I'm not willing to help *you* or think *you're* a waste of my time, it's that all of these menial little tasks that you guys ask me to fix can easily be remedied by someone else, and they *shouldn't* require my attention."

Here we were again, with our two completely different viewpoints coming to a head, and with this last statement, I realized that in order to continue functioning in our relationship, I had been compartmentalizing. Just as Matt was seeing supporting me and supporting our business as two very separate things, I had been separating our business disagreements with our romantic relationship in my mind. That is how we had been able to carry on living out our everyday lives still loving and respecting one another in the midst of these discussions without having any resolution. When we saw we were getting nowhere, we would give it a rest for a few days (or sometimes weeks or months), and I'd fold it up and shove it away into the "business discussion" compartment of my life. If I didn't do that, then I *would* take this personally as well, and *everything* would be at risk of crumbling. But then why, I asked myself, couldn't I do that with our actual business, separate it from myself?

At times, compartmentalizing wouldn't work, as we were living, working (at least trying to), eating, and sleeping together. Our differences of opinion or stress about work would overflow into our personal lives. This was usually Matt bringing something up while we were lying in bed. He would recount an interaction he had with one of the La Buena Vida employees that day, complain about ass time, or bring up one of his latest business ideas. I was getting better at identifying this and not heading down an emotionally charged road, especially at 9 p.m. "That is *not* turning me on," I would say, and we could laugh and move into the more loving aspect of our relationship.

Eventually I did give in to him building another hotel with his business partner, but this bomb, his idea of selling, was still smoking and the fumes had me taking a harder look at changing my exterior circumstances. *Was this still even the dream*? I had allowed Matt to build on and expand on my dream so much that it wasn't even recognizable anymore. This was *not* pineapples and beach bike rides! It was HR, accounting, computers, and administrative tasks! I didn't want to manage people, and I never imagined providing so many services to so many people. I had really tried to back off and incorporate more gratitude and my yoga "forget about your worries and your strife" mindset, but I felt I was up against too much.[28] So, was I ready to sell? What would that look like? How does that feel?

The truth is, even though Matt had completely aggrandized my original business plan, it had been consensual. I had allowed it, so

[28] Lyrics from the song The Bare Necessities written by Terry Gilkyson which was featured in the 1967 Disney animated film The Jungle Book

I couldn't really place all the blame on him. It had been obvious when we joined forces that we would need to do something beyond massage, but by allowing something other than my dream to unfold, I had become something I am not. I was no longer living heart first and this is where dis-ease had crept in. And oddly, what we created had somehow become my entire identity! I had been a hotel and restaurant owner to the very best of my ability for over eleven years. What would I do if I wasn't doing this? And was it fair for me to let go of what had become my entire identity because Matt had essentially outgrown it?

The longer I thought about it, the more I realized this was probably the only option. I had been doing the work on myself and relinquishing some of my responsibilities, but the bottom line was that even with managers, we were the owners of this business, and ultimately, it was our responsibility. If Matt truly was no longer up for participating as an owner because he viewed his time as being more valuable elsewhere, then La Buena Vida was too big of a responsibility for me on my own. Matt got shit done. Having built the place himself, he knew how everything worked and how to fix just about anything. There was no replacing him, and there was no one else I wanted to work alongside of. And I was tired. I didn't have the energy or the desire to. Still, a little part of my heart was breaking.

We talked, and it was obvious that he was less attached to La Buena Vida than I was. The health food menu, creating lunch specials, the yoga, and massage were all still my passions. As challenging as they sometimes were, I loved our employees too. Fausti had been with us for nearly twelve years now. The cooks had been working with us for many years too; one for ten years, the other for eight. The waitress three years. I loved our yoga studio with the beautiful hardwood floor and the wrought iron guardrail in the shape of all different yoga poses. There was nothing else like it. Our place was truly unique, and I cared deeply about it.

"Okay, if that's what you want, let's sell then," was his cold response, but it wasn't what I wanted. My first choice was for us to continue to run the business *together*. If that wasn't going to happen, I felt like I had no other choice then to sell. "I don't think that's in our best interest," he said.

I wasn't ready to list the hotel, and I didn't really want people to know we were selling. I wanted to feel heard and for Matt to see the big picture before we made what would be a monumental decision for *me*. My parents were in the process of moving from the Miami area to the gulf side of Florida and we were planning on going to visit and see their new house once they were settled. I looked for a couple's therapist in that area who could help mediate a healthier conversation about selling. Matt was reluctant. He didn't want to feel like a failure by admitting we needed help solving our problems, but I insisted that this would be a last stitch effort to see if we couldn't come up with any other solutions. I felt he owed me that much. There were a lot of tears on everyone's part (including the counselor's) because it was obvious that we really loved and respected one another. Matt maintained that we couldn't afford for him to solely work within our business. His career as a custom builder was taking off and therefore so was our income potential. I couldn't argue with that, but I was letting go of my dream so that he could pursue his career. I wanted him to understand that. We came up with no other solutions but being with the counselor allowed me to finally feel heard. And even though I still felt it was unfair, and a part of me was dying, I *reluctantly* agreed to put La Buena Vida on the market.

Chapter 23

Sympathetic Joy

We listed our business online with a very discreet realtor based in Belize. We knew it could be a slow process, but we were always meeting people in the restaurant who were looking to buy, and fair or unfair, making the decision to sell felt as if a giant weight had been lifted from me. We hardly told anyone because we knew a lot of people would be shocked or disappointed. Even though we were planning on staying in Joyita, there were friends and regular restaurant customers that wouldn't want us to sell for fear of us leaving or the restaurant closing. I didn't want other people's opinions to influence my headspace. I also didn't want to jinx a potential sale or have any of our employees quit because they heard the news. At times I would find myself waffling, especially when I saw family businesses that had kept the torch lit for generations and I'd wish I could do that.

In a sense, La Buena Vida Restaurant had become an institution. It was a reliable place for everyone to come hang out, and I loved providing that space, but underneath the surface of the relaxed and familiar atmosphere we were providing, I knew how much work it really was! I'd feel satisfied after a particular yoga class, retreat, or a great group came through, but I knew I was ready for this chapter, *no this volume*, of my life to be over. I would become sad if I thought about it from the perspective of giving up my dream, and I would sometimes question if I was somehow a failure for not being able to continue, but we *had* done it. We had achieved so much! Because of Matt, I had actually achieved far more than I had ever set out to do, and ironically, that was the problem.

I knew everything Matt was doing was because he wanted us to be financially successful, but I was still pushing back against the idea that money equals success. I knew I still wanted happiness, not success, to be at the top of my life's pyramid not some house on a hill. Sure, lots of people from the outside looking in would think I *was* successful, and in every practical sense, as a hotel and a restaurant owner in tropical paradise, I guess I was. This was an amazing accomplishment, but it was hardly a source of joy for me anymore, so it didn't really equate to success for me. We were starting to discuss moving to the little house as another way to take a giant step back from our business, and I wanted that. The problem was that even though this house was on the same hillside as La Buena Vida, it was further out of town towards the beach, and it was behind a gate, so to me it felt like we would be leaving the village for an uppity gated community. In my younger years, I could have never imagined this for myself, and now I began to question if I would somehow be compromising my core values by moving here.

There were only two other houses in addition to ours behind this gate, but it still looked and felt like a gated community to me. I undeniably had a judgment about gated communities, *especially* about expats who move to a foreign country to live in a gated community. In my mind, these people were intentionally closing themselves off to, and were possibly afraid of, the world around them that I had wanted so much to be a part of. In this stereotypical image I held, they didn't even speak the language, which was unthinkable to me! And it was one thing for me to judge other people, but I certainly didn't want to be judged, especially if none of these things were actually true.

Throughout my backpacking days, I had envisioned living in the tropics, but as a chronic weed smoker with my dreadlocks growing down to the ground. I had imagined I'd be living in the Blue Mountains in Jamaica, not like a blue haired retiree in a gated community. I knew I needed to start to dismantle this stereotype, as well as those I held about people with money if I wanted to feel good about this move and selling La Buena Vida.

I had been familiar with the saying, "Show me your friends, and I'll show you your future," meaning we are a product of the people we surround ourselves with. But it wasn't until this moment, and the fact that it felt like I was about to step into something much bigger than my previous belief system *and* the small village mentality of Joyita, that I took a hard look at how my environment and my relationships were impacting my life.[29] Besides Matt, hardly anyone was "thinking and growing rich" in this community.[30] In fact, just like the counterculture (and oftentimes the yoga/spiritual) community, the general sentiment in Joyita was that you cannot be a good person or spiritual if you have money. More than once it had been explained to me by people in the village that ambition was something to be leery of. *La ambición* translates directly in Spanish still meaning goal, aspiration, or urge. But on a *few* occasions, I was told that to be *ambicioso* (ambitious) meant to be greedy or want (aspire to) things you didn't have which was *not* a

[29] Quote attributed to Dan Peña, which was later incorporated in a *great* Pitbull/Stephen Marley song entitled Options.
[30] Reference to the book *Think and Grow Rich* by Napoleon Hill, The Ralston Society, 1937

good thing. Instead of our American culture that values and sees ambition as motivation, they related it to coveting and a lack of gratitude for what you do have.

As Matt and I started packing the bird cage up to finally move into the new house off-site, I felt lost. I was floating somewhere between my highly motivated self and my counter culture belief system that I was now seeing had been causing a "lack" or "scarcity mentality," just like it was for the majority in Joyita. I began to see moving as a way to create more distance; not only from our business, but space from the social atmosphere of the restaurant, and the overwhelming sentiment in the village which in addition to less is more, was also that having more made you less (of a good person).

We had hired a Panamanian manager from the city who we would house in our place, so we had begun taking our personal items out of the bird cage and the hotel in physical preparation for a complete transformation. I began clipping the plants that I loved and was transplanting them in our new yard, spending more time in *this* garden and tending to my own growing new perspectives. For the first time in over a decade, I truly had alone time, and I began to reconnect to nature; where I found peace, where I connected to spirit, to love, and to trust. I began to relax and to trust more. Trust myself, trust Matt and our decision, and trust our new manager to do his job in his own way. Having less interaction with the public helped me to be less reactionary and slowing down allowed more time and space to simply observe the world around me.

When I listened to friends, I realized that what I was mostly listening to was complaining and criticizing others. When people came by the restaurant to chat, they did just that, *they* chatted. They hardly listened and rarely asked how I was doing. Nearly everyone just went on and on about themselves and their perceived problems, as well as gossiped about other people. I began to notice that a lot of the gossip from both locals and foreigners was centered around other people's short comings or misfortunes. It had an entertaining undertone, as if they/*we* all took pleasure in seeing other people fail. When I spoke, I tried my best not to talk about others and to focus on the positive things we had going on in our lives. In seeing this, I understood that even though I didn't feel like I was my old positive-vibration-self, not to the degree that I once was, I was still attempting to lift up the people around me and I realized that they were bringing me down!

Another focal point of conversations was the growing negativity around a new demographic of people who were arriving in Joyita with more money to build second or third homes and open new businesses. It wasn't just the local town members who were anti-foreigners and development now; it was the foreigners and the developers as well. More people and businesses had the potential to threaten the underdeveloped way of life here, as well as threaten the success of established businesses with the general sentiment being, "if someone else is winning, then that means we are losing." I too had fallen into this trap, worrying about our quality of life and our business being in danger. Change was all around us now. Joyita had thirty-some other hotels and thirty-some other restaurants in operation so it was hard *not* to be concerned about our business. Even though I knew that thinking there wasn't enough business for everyone was scarcity mentality, I was still struggling to get myself back to living within the non-judgmental "sacred space" of not worrying what anybody else was doing. I dug in deeper as to *why* we feel so threatened by other people's success and how it actually serves us.

I began researching scarcity mentality and really going within and what I discovered was that if we label successful people as bad or greedy, it means that they are the "other" or separate from us. And "us broke-ass people" who are down here at the bottom struggling are somehow better *together*. Putting people down and complaining is a mini ego stroke that lifts us up and makes us feel better than "the other," at least temporarily. This camaraderie seemed to be the underlying sentiment throughout the community, which could be one of the greatest obstacles for breaking out of poverty, and what was making it difficult for me to break out of my old belief systems. I had found a sense of belonging by adopting a hippie mindset for so many years. I thought I was different. I wasn't "so American," the average tourist, and definitely not a rich gringa. Therefore, I/we were somehow better or other. But in my heart I knew we were all the same. We all have the same human desires to fit in, to be seen, and to do well for ourselves while we're here.

When I really stopped to think about it, I knew that having more "winning" businesses would bring more tourists and more commerce overall. I also saw that the more someone has, the more they are able to do and share, and that we actually need more good people in the world to be financially successful to help make positive change. Matt understood this. So did his partner, and some of the new or the "rich people" that everyone was outwardly hating on and inwardly feeling so threatened by. These were actually the movers and shakers with bigger ideas who had deeper pockets to make things happen in the community. They were helping to create events and donate land for parks and much needed public restrooms at the beach. They were working to establish the criteria for a responsible development plan for Joyita, but instead of focusing on the good they were doing, they were being criticized and perceived as "having too much." It had even been said that Matt and I "had too much," so now I asked myself why I should be ashamed of simply not wanting to get by anymore but wanting to thrive in all areas of my life.

I slowly began distancing myself from the people who I noticed were negative, and would openly take stabs at Matt and I. I looked around for examples of people who I considered to be progressive, spiritual, *and* rich, but there were very few in the vicinity. I decided to start picking peoples brains, but it became apparent quite quickly that no one I talked to had struggled with receiving money the way I did. I thought Hippie Matthew might have some insight for me being both spiritual and a successful business person, but he didn't seem to fully understand how heavy this weight had become for me. "Yeahhh well money is a funny thing mommy," he said, and after a few other side tangents eventually finished with, "You know what they say, *los ricos también lloran*," meaning the rich cry, too. So in the end, money doesn't really change all that much. Maybe I was just giving this way too much weight in my life???

Right when I felt I had reached a dead end with my self-inquiry, our visiting massage therapist and yoga instructor asked if I would be available to participate in her Thai-Yoga Massage training to receive massages from her students. Taking part in the wellness activities was one of the amazing benefits of owning a yoga studio that I knew I would miss once we sold our business. I agreed and arrived early to receive the beginning of her training which she had encouraged me to do. She opened by sharing what are referred to as the four immeasurables (or boundless qualities) in Buddhism and explained how love (*metta*) and compassion (*karuna*) are the qualities most discussed and understood. She then went on to explain the concept of *mudita* or sympathetic joy at length which I had never heard of. She told us that it's widely believed that only through mudita can we genuinely feel love and compassion towards others. In a fun role play, she demonstrated how often times we aren't happy for others' success because they have something we wanted for ourselves. If the surf is good and we missed it; or we weren't at the big party; or we see a friend with a new partner, instead of feeling sympathetic joy and being happy for their good fortune, we end up feeling sorry for ourselves. "Mudita is essentially being happy for other peoples' successes," which she explained, "can be very difficult at times and even a rarity in this world." She talked about mudita being the antidote to envy, coveting, and taking pleasure in other peoples' failures. This was huge and exactly what I needed to hear in that moment! She led us through a meditation where she invited us to send love and happiness to others, especially those we felt were doing "better than" us. I was glowing as I sent love to those people and businesses that I had been feeling challenged and threatened by. I felt gratitude that these tools and teachings were still making their way into my life and that I now had something I could work with. This gave me a glimpse of the kind of transformation that can come from truly feeling happy for other people, especially those who we may feel we are in competition with. I realized these were the magic ingredients of sacred space, that when we are *happy* and feeling *secure* within ourselves, we do not worry about what other people are doing *or* feel threatened by their success. This was what I needed to anchor into, more of my own joy and what makes me happy. I began sending everything up into the Universe; my prayers, my gratitude, my messages that I *was* truly ready to sell our business, and that I was ready to receive this money. I stepped into that, began walking in that, and then eventually, felt I was living in that as my truth.

Chapter 24

The Beginning

When I thought about what I would do *when* (not if) we sold our business, I mostly thought about massage and yoga. Since I loved the studio, I would be happy to continue to support the wellness program at La Buena Vida, and I definitely wanted to keep creating art. I didn't know if that would be a possibility with these new owners that I was now actively working to attract. So, I began to ask myself what completely reinventing myself would look like, and I came up with writing. I had always wanted to write a book about my early psychedelic and travel adventures, and if it inspired other people to create their own reality, then even better. High speed Internet had finally arrived in Joyita, and now as I worked on a new art piece for La Buena Vida up at the house, I began to listen to podcasts. It was 2018, and it was really the first time that I had more free time and access to books and conversations online about spirituality, abundance, and the 'psychedelic renaissance' that was now underway with the therapeutic use of psychedelics becoming more mainstream. As I made more time for the things I loved, I felt more joy and happiness resurfacing in my life, and my heart began to open to limitless possibilities yet again.

I was grateful for this new little reprieve at the house where because of the gate and the steep climb, no one ever dropped in unexpectedly, and I felt grateful that Matt had continued pushing me to get it. As different as we were, I was making an active effort to release my judgment and not criticize our differences, but actually appreciate them. I began to realize that he really was just trying to achieve a greater quality of life for us, and we *did* balance each other out. He had pushed me forward into a more comfortable lifestyle after having lived in a 300 square foot birdcage for *six years*. And I was reeling him in so that he slowed down enough to enjoy this lifestyle we had created for ourselves and the ocean view we now had, together. Interestingly, when we took a Myers-Briggs personality test, we discovered we have the exact same personality type, we are ENFPs (Extraverted, Intuitive, Feeling, Prospecting); free-spirited creatives! As mind-blowing as this was, it made sense because I knew that we were both always looking to grow, but his growth was usually more financial and mine more personal and spiritual. Matt had always put me on a pedestal and admired and respected our differences. It was *me* that was finding my way back to that place and letting go of him needing to change, to be more spiritual, or have my exact same belief system. Thank God, I thought, that he didn't, or we might still be living in the hut!

I've believed that we are all here to learn different lessons, and now I was realizing that someone doesn't have to be "spiritual" to learn. It was obvious that Matt had mastered accepting abundance and not taking things personally or caring what other people think, the things that I was still grappling with. And truthfully, for as much as I preached about the importance of altruism to him, and I may have been more generous with my time, he's definitely a lot more fluid with money than I am. When we bought a new truck, he basically gave Bobo (the local guy he works with) the busito and helped him to get a driver's license. He's given countless surfboards to kids who he knew were learning to surf, but didn't have a board. He would always say that we arrived to Joyita with backpacks, and we could leave with backpacks. So I knew that his quest for financial success was not all about material gain. It was more about freedom, and I was definitely down with that.

We were learning to dance around our differences by focusing on understanding and respecting our conflicting viewpoints while not trying to change one another's minds or convince the other we were right. We had come to realize that with some things, that was *never* going to happen anyway! I maintained that we came here for quality of life, and that we didn't need to worry so much about our finances because The Universe would provide. Matt would say that *he* is that person in the universe that's providing for us. We were able to laugh and acknowledge our differing perspectives, but that didn't necessarily "fix" anything. At times, we were still unable to move forward when it came to big decision making regarding business or investments.

Despite its rough edges, I was still grateful for having settled in Joyita. When Matt and I first arrived it called to us because it was an authentic village, much like the destinations and experiences I had always been drawn to throughout the adventures of my youth. There wasn't a pretentious vibe that we felt in other yoga-esoteric-dance-party-wellness type *overdeveloped* destinations. It felt like a down to earth, humble, fishing community, essentially a tropical Kodiak. We had no idea what living here would entail or that we would be part of so many growing pains, but just like our relationship, I've learned a lot from adversity. If and when I thought back to those first few weeks in Joyita and wondered if we had purchased too quickly or blindly, I had no regrets because I knew that, "wherever you go, there you are."[31] I truly believe we would have experienced some sort of culture clash wherever we decided to relocate. My experiences also taught me that it's healthy to constantly question your own beliefs and values. For me, Joyita may have come to be our place because we *were* both equipped to handle the discomfort of change, which really was inevitable. And maybe it was just wishful thinking, but I'd like to believe that by my being here and establishing a business with an emphasis on health and wellness, I could have inspired others in some way and possibly helped to influence the direction of Joyita's development.

I still didn't feel completely accepted by the local population, in fact, I knew that if I was looking to be considered a local, that was *never* going to happen. This became apparent when I would hear Fausti say things like, "*Ustedes como extranjeros*," (you guys, as foreigners) as he drew a figurative line in the sand trying to explain our differences. I realized that if even he, after so many years of having worked together and being part of one another's families saw us as separate, then pretty much everyone saw us in that light.

---

[31] Quote credited to Thomas à Kempis written in *The Imitation of Christ* originally published in Medieval Latin in the early 1400s

But that was okay. I *wasn't* from here, and over the years our differences had become obvious to me as well. Just like Matt, that didn't mean I wasn't able to appreciate those differences. I still loved Fausti, the culture here, and all the little idiosyncrasies of this place that I now call home.

It was right when I knew that I *was* absolutely (more than) ready for change that we finally had a couple who was seriously interested in buying our business. They were not health and wellness people, but she was a chef and a foodie and the restaurant would be her focus whereas the restaurant was my least favorite aspect of our business. I had *some* yoga guilt about potentially not selling to wellness people, as the studio was so beautiful. Together with the hotel, it had lots of retreat potential, but they were open to me continuing to be involved in the wellness aspect of the business. *And*, I told myself, I had wanted to sell and had been sending my messages up to The Universe, and this was the opportunity and the people who were sent to us. They were also Americans, more Matt's age in their early fifties, who we shared a lot of other common interests with. In fact, whenever we sat down with them, we would talk for hours. Not just about our business, but about life in Panamá, gardening, plants, food, travel, kids, etcetera so this felt right.

Making the decision to give up La Buena Vida taught me that I can't always get what I want, but this certainly did seem like what I needed.[32] This was a *compromise* which (like my dad had told Matt years ago), was the secret to a successful, happy (maybe those two

---

[32] The Rolling Stones, "You Can't Always Get What You Want," track #9 on Let It Bleed, Decca/London, 1969

can be synonymous) marriage. As the sale looked like it was getting closer to becoming a reality, I prepared to throw myself into the place that I loved once again. The place I had always thrived, and that had been lost to me for some time now. I was slowly making my way back into the unknown.

The Beginning

End Note

A ReAwakening is a personal memoir wherein everything did in fact happen and was shared as I recalled it, to the best of my ability. I did, however, piece some events out of chronological order where they would be more easily explained, served to build context, and create fluidity. Because music has been such a huge part of my life, particular songs I included here *did* actually play in my head in some moments. Others that were influential in my life, but may have not been recalled in that particular space in time were sprinkled throughout. Nearly all the names have been changed out of respect for people's privacy, as well as some places, including Joyita, as this was my personal experience living here and most of the incidents I shared happen many moons ago before it became the popular tourist destination that it is today.

A Special Thanks

To my husband "Matt" first and foremost whose name *was* changed as well, for reasons that may or may not become more apparent in Book #3. I applaud us both for continuing to try, to grow, and learn on our journey together. I thank him for his willingness to allow me to share as much I did about him and our relationship. Thank you to my parents whose community-mindedness, hard work, and can-do attitude did finally wear off on me. Thanks to Hippie Matthew, all his "Matthewisms," and supportive friendship over the years, as well as other "Joyita" friends, both new and old, who've shared the experience of living in such a different culture, so far at the end of the road, together. To Amy Kochek who as my editor, forced me to extract and share more of my internal journey on these pages. And to all you all for taking this journey with me and your continued love and support!

Questions for Self-Reflection

1. At times my free-spirited nature led me into some "unusual" situations. Have you lived your life in a similar way, risk taking and "going with the flow" or are you a "planner?" How have you benefited from these traits and where could you stand to either grow or reel yourself in a bit more?
2. A huge part of my journey has been my resistance to the system which largely stemmed from the belief that "money is bad." What is your relationship with money and/or receiving? Are there other belief systems that you've adopted that may be limiting your growth in some way?
3. In hindsight, we probably rushed into purchasing property in Panamá, though sometimes you've just "gotta do the thing." Is there anything in your life you may have stepped into "too fast?" How has it affected you and what were the blessings or lessons you received from that experience?
4. A great deal of my growth came through my relationship with Matt; our conflicting perspectives and our struggle to respect those differences. Does this dynamic exist in any of your significant relationships? Have you been able to find mutual resolve or internal resolution? If so, how? -please let me know.
5. I wrote about the three ways we learn (through divine grace, experience, or suffering). Which one of these do you feel has been most prevalent in your life? Which one do you feel you've grown the most from?

6. The spiritual aspect of yoga is what brought me back to having a spiritual experience here on Planet Earth. What (if any) practices do you use intentionally to honor life and connect with your higher self/God/The Universe? Is there a practice that interests you that you would like to make more time for?

7. Many times in my life it has occurred to me that negativity, gossip, and criticism are not unique to "Joyita" or village life. In fact, talking about our problems seems to be the societal go-to when it comes to conversation. Are you able to express sympathetic joy for others and do you have positive and supportive people in your life? Name them.

8. Several times in *A ReAwakening* I wrote about creating change in my life by adjusting my internal environment and shifting my perspective, but as the stakes got higher, I found that increasingly more challenging. I finally had to make changes to affect my external circumstances. Have you seen evidence in your own life where changing your perspective did change the world around you? How are you able to tell when you need to take external action to change the world around you?

9. Is there something your heart has been calling you to do? What's stopping you?

Made in the USA
Middletown, DE
15 October 2023

40864958R00163